Matthew Campling is a qualified psychotherapist. Matthew was an advice writer (agony uncle) for various publications for ten years.

In addition to radio appearances and writing magazine articles he was a regular guest expert on ITV's 'Trisha' show in 2001 & 2002. He has also had seven stage plays performed, in South Africa and London. He works in private practice in Islington, London, and lives in London and Lincolnshire. He facilitates an ongoing programme of therapeutic workshops for a variety of organisations including London's Central YMCA.

Eating Disorder Self Cure:
The Matthew Method

by

Matthew Campling

**Grosvenor House
Publishing Limited**

Matthew Campling is hereby identified as author of this
work in accordance with Section 77 of the Copyright, Designs
and Patents Act 1988

The book cover picture is copyright to Matthew Campling

This book is published by
Grosvenor House Publishing Ltd
28-30 High Street, Guildford, Surrey, GU1 3HY.
www.grosvenorhousepublishing.co.uk

A CIP record for this book
is available from the British Library

ISBN 978-1-906210-51-9

For HSH

Contents

CONTENT

CHAPTER ONE

Background

> '*What is an eating disorder?*
> *It is a defence mechanism of the body that has gone terribly wrong.*
> *How do you recover from an eating disorder?*
> *By realising that you are not it. By separating, then negotiating with the disorder, as you gradually take back its energy and regrow your healthy self.*'

This idea is the essence of my approach and what makes it different from other methods of responding to eating disorders. Whatever the situation – whether underweight or overweight - my own personal experience and original thinking, information from other therapeutic sources and the ongoing results of my work with clients has caused me to believe in the truth of the above statement. So crucial do I believe this idea to be that I have quoted it from the chapter that follows this one.

In all my speaking to people with both kinds of disorders I have not encountered anyone who does not see the simplicity and validity of the above. But recovery is not as simple as this, so this book will provide more of what seems to be crucial for recovery.

This book can be read by someone who believes they have a disorder, or someone close to someone in that situation, or by a member of the medical, psychiatric or therapeutic professions seeking to add to their understanding. Because I offer the book to professionals who are used to academically referenced texts I have done so here. But if you are reading this as someone with an eating disorder, or a carer, then it will be easier to concentrate on the thread of original thinking that makes up my

'D-I-Y' approach.

May I suggest, if you are someone with a disorder, particularly anorexia, that you attempt just a little at a time. In order to really absorb what is being presented, just a couple of pages, or less, will give a better result. The first time I read a psychological book, I used to lie on my bed and read a couple of pages, then fall asleep! Then when I woke up I'd read a little more. But in this way I was able to really absorb what was on the page.

This self-published edition marks the first year of my ongoing work with clients with eating disorders. I have self-published because I did not want to wait the time that it takes for conventional publishing. It is very much a document about early days, about experimenting with ideas and observing what works in practice.

One difference between myself and most other professionals in this field is that I have experienced both overweight and under-weight myself. Specifically when I had anorexia, in the absence of any other resources, I had to look deep inside myself, come to a profound realisation as to the nature of the disorder, and find a way to cure myself.

However this book is not primarily about me. Clients have taken my ideas and tried them out for what works for them. The feedback has helped me to define, refine and understand ever more deeply aspects of the cause and cure of an eating disorder. This book is therefore a chronicle of a number of individuals' honest, internal, struggle and growth.

This book was written during the Spring, Summer and Autumn of 2007. In the new academic year (October) I began a two-year, part-time MA in Eating Disorders at a prominent thera-peutic and teaching institution. Many of the quotes from eating disorder literature contained in the book I have come across in the course of my extensive background reading. However I am not seeking primarily to present a comprehensive overview of academic literature, but to set down my original thinking.

A major reason for writing this book is to lay out the very concept of an 'eating disorder self-cure'. It is written to be an addition to the current literature and methods of cure. There is already a great deal of literature on the subject and much being done in the field of eating disorders. Therefore this book is not a challenge or an argument. It is offered as an augmentation to present understanding. It is my contribution, another addition to the vast scope of what is already being accomplished.

Then why is this book needed? Because in all my reading I haven't come across anyone working in exactly the same way as me. As the beginning of the chapter states, I have come to believe that an eating disorder is a *mechanism*, an aspect of the body's defence system that has gone horribly wrong. Therefore it needs a different approach to really engage with the reality of what has taken place within the psyche and the physical body. My vision is for the information in this book to be *integrated* into the mainstream of academic understanding and recovery programmes.

But that is only *my* wish – your wish may be more simple: to find relief from the pain of anorexia, bulimia or overweight. So I write this book specifically for you, the person who is now where I once was. At stages in my life I have been miserably overweight, and drastically underweight. I have lived to tell the tale – and what follows documents a voyage into understanding the relationship between ourselves, the food we eat or deny ourselves, those around us who are also affected, and the whole of our daily lives.

When I began my exploration, I thought of eating disorders as involving underweight only. A chance question when I was presenting early research, and then the opportunity of working with a highly motivated individual, widened my understanding to include overweight. As you will see, I have separated the overweight section from the underweight, since they were developed separately, and in the first section I refer to 'eating disorders' solely as affecting underweight, since otherwise it will be confusing for someone interested in one end of the line to keep being referred to the other end.

That overweight *also* seems to be a disorder I explore in the second section. The two sections can be read independently. Although because there are obvious similarities, reading the book as a whole will further enhance your understanding of what we mean by an 'eating disorder'.

I would like to acknowledge three people who have supported the beginnings of my exploration. My former supervisor, Hazel Burnett, was the first person to share my awakening understanding. Mike Worrall, a distinguished person-centred editor and lecturer, and my present supervisor, has commented on several drafts of the book. Leah Davidson, my own therapist, has listened to the interface between my personal and work lives.

When attempting to venture into unknown territory it is crucial to feel that one is not working alone. I have also appreciated the support of all the people who have responded to the early writings on my website. Supported by their feedback and encouragement I have the confidence to set down what follows.

Section One

Underweight

CHAPTER TWO

Definition

If you are starting the book here it is important that you are aware of the style in which it is written. Some information is repeated.

You may not need to have this, but in my experience people with an eating disorder gain by hearing the same information repeated. Please overlook the repetition if it is not helpful to you.

What is an eating disorder?

It is a defence mechanism of the body that has gone terribly wrong.

How do you recover from an eating disorder?

By realising that you are not it. By separating, then negotiating with the disorder, as you gradually take back its energy and re-grow your healthy self.

That's why this book is called 'self-cure'. Because the person who has a disorder doesn't need – in fact it is often the opposite of helpful – others to insist that they eat. If you are the one with an eating disorder, it won't help to be told that you are stubborn, or spiteful – 'why won't you make us happy by eating?' It is not the most supportive approach to have your spirit broken by an onslaught of well-meaning professionals. I would like to suggest that what may be more helpful is the information in this book, and then the right support to effect your own recovery from your disorder.

The *concept* of the patient or client being in charge is widely supported. Donald Winnicott writes: 'Psychotherapy is not making clever and apt interpretations; by and large it is a long-term giving the patient back what the patient brings. I like to think of my work in this way, and I think that if I do this well enough the patient will find his or her own self, and will be able to exist and to feel real' (Winnicott, 1971p. 117).

But, of course, without understanding the core nature of a disorder, recovery work will take, at least, much longer, and ultimately may never have the completeness that would come from truly disengaging the Eating Disorder Mechanism (EDM).

I will go on to expand on what I mean by an EDM. For now, let me explain how it is that I've come to this understanding. My approach has taken years to come together. Partly it's been my own experience, partly pieces of the jigsaw garnered from sources inside and outside the therapeutic mainstream, partly from the experience and feedback of clients.

I am now a psychotherapist, working predominantly with people with eating disorders. However, thirty years ago, I had anorexia. (This was after having been overweight as a child, as I will detail further in the second section).

Beginning at 17, I dropped from eleven and a half stone to, at 20 and a half, six stone six pounds. At that point I had a partial breakdown – basically I started crying at work and couldn't stop. Just at the moment when I finally acknowledged to myself that I was seriously ill, I also became aware that I was not in charge of my eating.

It was a desperate situation. At that time, in the country where I was living (Durban, South Africa), there were no resources. Not the sort that can be trusted, the only solution mooted by the GP being 'electro shock-therapy' (this was a behavioural method that gained some popularity before being discredited through its poor results (Garner, 1968)).

I knew I was ill. My exhausted mind constantly yearned for bed and oblivion. My body ached and pleaded for rest. My emotional self was terrified of the despair that was my future. I finally acknowledged that if I didn't find a way to pull myself back from the brink of death, I would, logically, die.

With no other resources I looked inside myself and found the answer. Somehow, even in my depleted state, I still retained a small, weak, healthy part. And it still had a trick. This weak part, my

David if you like, began to negotiate with the Goliath that was the powerful, merciless disorder – the disorder manifestation I now call the Eating Disorder Mechanism (EDM).

This is how it worked for me. I knew this thing inside me was fanatically devoted to exercise. On a typical day I would wake up and immediately exercise, then at lunch time go swimming outside in all weathers, and at night, after the most insignificant of meals or more likely nothing at all I would return to my bedroom in my parents' house and exercise. And then falling into bed I would, more often than not, not so much fall asleep as black out.

I well knew this thing inside's passion for exercise. So I made a deal with it. In order to be able to exercise, I needed fuel. It therefore needed to let me eat – the amount would need to be negotiated – so that then I would be able to exercise.

You should understand that this was not a case of two distinct personalities sitting down to talk a point through. This was all taking place inside me. My negotiating with the disorder was partly accomplished through my thinking mind, through my emotions and it all took place within my physical body. And it worked.

In retrospect I have more fully appreciated my good fortune in living in that seaside town. My parents' house was a mile away from the University swimming pool. Although I had no legal right to use the pool, I was there so early in the morning that there was no one else around to question my presence. Walking to the pool along quiet roads bursting with Durban's sub-tropical foliage, feeling the sweet cool morning air on my skin, diving into the mysterious and refreshing water was itself enormously important in my healing process.

Afterwards I would prepare a meal before leaving for work. This was my home-made fruit parfait. Layers of cereal, yoghurt, fruit. Gradually I was able to include more solid cereal, less fruit. At lunch time I continued to leave the office where I was working and walk quickly to the swimming pool where I was the still the brownest and thinnest of swimmers. But I did eat a proper sandwich. And sometimes I was able to eat at night, a habit I had dropped a couple of years previously.

I remember the first time in years I ate a baked potato served with butter. I can describe the experience only as like having little golden fireworks go off in my mouth. My poor, deprived taste buds were taking no chances that I would not get the point – that *this* was the sort of food it craved (Campling, 2006).

I also remember, while swimming one morning, turning at the end of the pool and coming up with my long hair in my eyes. The morning sun, rising in the East, was caught by the droplets of water in my hair. It was like miniature suns briefly held and dancing, dancing as I swam. I remember laughing out loud in delight, because I could feel inside me the *energy* to laugh. Because I knew that part of my laughter was coming from a sense of hope, that the answer I had instinctively fallen upon was working: *I was coming back to life.*

Once I had recovered my faculties – once the energy of the disorder had passed back into my healthy self – I got on with my life. So totally did I forget my anorexic period that people who came to know me over the years have been surprised, in the last couple of years, to hear it had ever been an issue.

I think I was frightened. I think forgetting about it meant I didn't have to confront how close I had come to my own death. It was only several years ago, when I attended a workshop on eating disorders, that I acknowledged this period of my history.

The woman who ran the workshop declared at one point: 'I don't work with anorexics unless they promise to eat normally'. Instantly my reaction was that this was terribly wrong. That the very worst thing you could do to an anorexic or bulimic was to force them to eat 'normally'. In fact the workshop was so painful to experience that again I stopped thinking about eating disorders. I wasn't yet ready. It was still too personal.

I was finally able to face my past – and begin to look at how my experience might be shared – on Christmas Eve 2005. While other people were preparing for Christmas, I was agonising. This was because I had just read published reports on work with eating disorders (BACP 2005). It wasn't so much what they said, but how – given my experience – there was something crucial, in my opinion, that was not being included.

9

Having so much insightful research available, but also believing that the body of literature might benefit from my own recovery process, I felt obliged to share my own experience. So on that Christmas Eve I sat down and wrote 2,000 words on what it had been like for me. Some of it is contained in the paragraphs above. Even then, I found it so painful to have to look back in detail that I needed to wait a couple of weeks before I could read back what I had written.

I sent this off to the BACP (British Association of Counselling and Psychotherapy of which I am an Accredited member) for consideration in our house journal, Therapy Today. It was published in June 2006. I received over 40 positive and enthusiastic responses. I was asked to write the chapter on eating disorders in a book on client-centred practice (Campling 2007). And it gave me the encouragement to pursue my own exploration.

It also brought me my first clients with eating disorders. Working with my clients, over the months, has been an invaluable aid in my developing and understanding more about what I believe an eating disorder to be. And how to effect a recovery.

I set up a website – *www.eatingdisorderself-cure.com*. As well as my early original thinking, the original article published in Therapy Today is reproduced. The site has brought me into contact with people from around the country and in fact the world. Through my connection with *beat*, the eating disorders association, I talk about my theories with the British media.

From that tentative beginning, encouraged by the responses I get from people with disorders, I now wish to set down where my approach is at the moment. I believe I understand the nature of the disorder in an original and *practical* way. What is true for the individual is often also true for the universal. I don't believe that I am unique or that my eating disorder functioned or was fashioned in a different way from anyone else.

Therefore I offer my observations so far, asking that, surely, what has worked for some must also have relevance and application to the many other people affected? At the moment the issue of eating disorders has never been more public – although that's also true for many other issues. Perhaps it's the stress of modern times, perhaps it's the proliferation of the media, which needs interesting, unusual stories. Sad stories of models who have died from unusual diets or young women who appear to have everything starving themselves have drawn the public's attention and imagination. This has both publicised, and complicated, the situation for the many people who are not models but whose life is affected by an eating disorder.

According to Shipton (2004) Anorexia nervosa is described in the ICD 10 (International Statistical Classification of Diseases and Related Health Problems (10th Revision), classification of Mental and Behavioural Disorders) as 'deliberate weight loss, induced and/or sustained by the patient' (WHO, 1992). For a definite diagnosis, all the following are required:

- Body weight is maintained at least 15 per cent below that expected either because it has been lost or never achieved
- Weight loss is achieved by avoiding fattening foods. One or more of the following self-induced strategies should be present: vomiting, purging, excessive exercise, use of appetite suppressants and/or diuretics
- There is endocrinal disorder leading to amenorrhoea in women and loss of potency or sexual interest in men. There may be elevated levels of growth hormone and cortisol, changes in thyroid hormone and abnormalities of insulin secretion
- If onset is before puberty, development is delayed or arrested and growth ceases so that girls do not develop breasts and there is primary amenorrhoea, and in boys the genitals remain juvenile. With recovery, puberty is often completed normally but girls may have their first period delayed.

If all the above are *not* in place, a definition of EDNOS (Eating Disorder Not Otherwise Specified) (Palmer 2001) may be made. There has, historically, also been a question about whether men can be classified as having anorexia nervosa since amenorrhoea (loss of menstrual cycle) obviously is not possible. However I believe men should be included because 'loss of potency and sexual interest' can include the disappearance of nocturnal emissions ('wet dreams') (Campling 2007).

Hilda Bruch, the distinguished American psychoanalyst, published The Golden Cage in 1978. She chose that title to highlight the most unusual aspect of the illness: seemingly it affected only offspring of the privileged. Nowadays that is no longer true although eating disorders are still unknown in some parts of Africa and Asia. Bruch's comment that 'about 25% of anorexic youngsters go through the binge-eating syndrome and may get stuck in it' (Bruch, 1978, p. 4) indicates that at the time bulimia was not treated as a separate illness.

'My stomach is like a paper bag – whatever I put in it just sits there and makes me feel ill' (1978, p.83) – nowadays we would call this bulimia, not anorexia. Bruch further notes that 'relatively little is known how this changeover takes place, from what looks like an ordinary dieting to this inflexible self-destructive but hotly defended fixation on weight and food' (p. 72).

Here she neatly defines what has always caused great anguish on both sides of the eating disorder issue – the person with the illness, and those who love them or who are trying to help them recover. There seems to be no explanation for the madness of an eating disorder. When food is abundant, when the facilities of a hospital or a psychotherapist are offered – why does the person insist on the 'self-destructive but hotly defended fixation'?

The answer – and the overall perspective of this book – is that the person is not in charge. The Eating Disorder Mechanism (EDM) is running the individual's life. What this means, and how to affect a recovery which works *with* this reality rather than in conflict with it, I will detail in the chapters to follow.

'The trouble is you are only available for 50 minutes a day and I need someone inside me all the time, therefore it has to be myself'. These words, noted by Marion Burgner (1997, p. 98) define the reason why I am pursuing an 'eating disorder self-cure'. The patient Burgner writes about was receiving analysis five times a week. But even having all the experience and skill of a highly committed professional for a set period wasn't enough: therefore I offer my approach with clients as an alternative.

Unlike analysts I am not schooled in interpreting clients' material from a Freudian or Kleinian perspective. Therefore I do not try to interpret their world. I offer my perspective and my growing knowledge based on clients' experiences and they grow by taking what works for them and, in a real sense, becoming their own therapist.

However, that is not to say I do not see the great value in an understanding of the analytical approach. Sigmund Freud's daughter Anna writes (1946, p120): 'Much of the child's conflicting behaviour towards food does not originate from loss of appetite or a lessened need to eat... but from conflicting emotions towards the mother which are transferred on to the food which is a symbol for her. Ambivalence towards the mother may express itself as fluctuations between over-eating and refusal of food; guilty feelings towards the mother and a consequent inability to enjoy her affection as an inability to enjoy food; obstinacy and hostility towards the mother as a struggle against being fed'.

I quote the above not to emphasise the role of the mother, but to show how long people have understood that behaviour and emotions are involved.

At first, the analytical approach may seem daunting. Even a brief dip into the brilliant – but challenging – writings of Melanie Klein bears out this statement (Klein 1921 – 1965). In fact I am dwelling on it only because it is the preferred approach within a hospital or psychiatric institution. Since I am presenting an alternative, I offer my work humbly, aware that I don't want to tread on toes.

My position in some ways is analogous to Minuchin (1978) writing in Psychosomatic Families. He was presenting the idea of 'systems therapy' – a family-oriented approach rather than concentrating on the individual. Mindful of how this might go over with colleagues favouring the traditional, individual approach he notes: *'Unfortunately, investigations of anorexia nervosa have demonstrated, to a startling degree, the blinders imposed on the scientist by his conceptual model. Practitioners maintain their previously learned paradigms as though they were causes to be defended, not hypotheses to be tested.*

'Thomas S Kuhn, in examining this tendency of researchers to cling to existing models and to resist change, concluded that the scientist's vision is severely restricted because 'to an extent unparalleled in most fields, they have undergone similar educations and professional initiations; in the process they have absorbed the same technical literature and drawn many of the same lessons from it. Usually the boundaries of that standard literature mark the limits of a scientific subject matter'.

'Much of the success of the scientific community in fact derives from its willingness to defend its shared assumptions – or 'normal science' in Kuhn's terminology – 'if necessary at considerable cost'. Normal science, for example, often suppresses fundamental novelties because they are necessarily subversive to its basic commitments. 'But', Kuhn suggests, when the profession 'can no longer evade the anomalies that subvert the existing tradition of scientific practice – then begins the extraordinary investigations that lead the profession at last to a new set of commitments, a new basis for the practice of science'. His formulation bears considerable relevance to the history of anorexia nervosa' (pgs 19 & 20).

Interestingly, Menuchin now would have no problem – the systems or family approach is widely used (eg, Dare, 1993). Now it's me who finds himself in the position of coming forward with a new idea, and hoping it will be embraced, not rejected.

With all that is already available, why bother to attempt to strike a new chord? For me, the following quote from Marianne Bentovim (2000, p. 351) is more persuasive than I could ever be: 'In Holland there has been some anecdotal reports of young women who have insisted on the right to die and effectively requested euthanasia, rather than prolong their suffering, both from anorexia nervosa, and the gruelling process of treatment'.

I believe there is an alternative to the 'gruelling process of treatment', one that works with the patient or client, and does not try to break them down, or beat the disorder into submission.

Before we leave 'definition', there follows a list of symptoms that people with anorexia or bulimia may be experiencing. The purpose of the list is to highlight the difference between someone who is unnaturally thin for reasons other than an eating disorder. For example, a young man I met presented with all the physical symptoms of anorexia – skeletal face, unnatural body thinness, the odd smell that has been widely commented on – but he had had Hepatitis C. Running through the list that follows, it took only a few questions for me to realise he definitely did *not* have anorexia.

This list can be read by someone who believes they may have a disorder, or someone who knows or works with people in that category.

Please note that *not identifying* with all of these does not mean anything specific. I have compiled the two lists from personal observation as well as the comments of clients and others. It is not intended to be exhaustive or definitively exclusive. Because it focuses only on anorexia and bulimia it does not include the idea of an ED-NOS – Eating Disorder Not Otherwise Specified – but it may still help the individual to understand more about what is going on inside them. The idea behind the list is to *open the lines of communication* – if you recognise yourself even in part or it makes sense of what appears to be happening to someone else, then it may be that you and I have begun the process of understanding – and the beginning of recovery.

Pointers towards Anorexia

- Food – and doing without – forms the core of your thinking every day.
- Your body is always hungry for exercise. You use exercise as a way of expressing yourself and feeling calm.
- When in a public place there is always something inside you, telling you to be on your own and exercise.
- The 'person' who most understands you is the inner voice that constantly talks about exercise and avoiding food
- Your body is often exhausted yet something inside you wants to drain even the last bit of energy through exercise
- You are always looking for little times to rest because you are always exhausted
- Relationships of any sort, sexual or otherwise, feel like an unwelcome interruption to the one you're having with yourself.
- When you do eat you can't help over-eating because it's like a floodgate of desire
- You know the calorific content of everything and you try to burn up more calories in little ways – ie – sitting impossibly straight, going up flights of stairs rather than using the elevator.
- You have developed a method for blocking out people who make inappropriate remarks about how thin you are or who appear upset by your thinness.
- You can't imagine that there could ever be another way of relating to food rather than the full-on way you have.
- You avoid public and other situations where food will be served. Christmas and festive periods are particularly difficult because you know you can't just relax and enjoy yourself.
- You only feel safe and happy when you're in your own room either about to exercise, exercising or post-exercise
- Eating food is wrong. There's a voice or a feeling inside you that tells you it is a terribly bad thing to do.

- When you do eat food it tends to be in a hurried, scrappy way where you just shove it down and rush off somewhere (ie basically avoiding the issue).
- You feel superior to other people because they are controlled by food whereas you are in charge.
- Sometimes you think you're on a treadmill and you don't know how to get off.

Pointers towards Bulimia

- You don't feel confident about your ability to keep food down –you just don't know how it works.
- Food seems foreign to your stomach.
- No one understands you as well as the inner voice that tells you vomiting is the only way to be secure.
- Other people get angry because they don't understand you can't be any other way.
- Selecting food is endlessly enjoyable because whatever you eat you know can only come up again.
- You don't tolerate the easy way. Things need to be tackled head on and they are always painful.
- Cleaning up after you have been ill is the only thing that makes you feel good about yourself. For the rest you are clearly a bad person.
- You don't trust your breathing or your ability to swallow and believe you need to have these things under your conscious control.
- Going out to a restaurant is to be avoided because you can't go through your enjoyable or unavoidable routine.
- The only way to maintain an even weight is to throw up what you eat.
- You hide from people the extent to which you believe you are ill because you don't want them to panic.
- You have noticed the relationship between your vomiting and emotional aspects of your life. When you've been wrong, you need to be punished.
- You feel superior to most people because you are so much harder on yourself.
- You control all the emotional aspects of your life by vomiting up the bad feelings.
- Sometimes you 'wake up' and feel frightened about what is going on inside you.
- In company you feel like everybody but you is having a great time while you feel unable to explain yourself.

- You wish your mother would sort herself out.
- You enjoy the control you have over food. While other people moan about diets, you merely regurgitate.
- You have regrets about relationships and friendships and give yourself a hard time because you deserve it.
- You've given up trying to explain how you work inside because people just give you stupid advice.
- You can't imagine anything beyond the way you live at the moment. The idea that food wouldn't be the centre of your day is unthinkable.
- You get frightened about what you might be doing to yourself.
- You can't help shouting - people don't understand.

CHAPTER THREE

Cause

Obviously it is essential to base any recovery on the most specific and realistic understanding of the nature of the disorder.

Whether a person is deemed Anorexic, Bulimic, a Bulimic Anorexic or an Anorexic Bulimic or a normal-weight Bulimic (Shipton 2004, Farrell, 2007), what is important is the blueprint of what it is we are dealing with. From Freud onwards theorists have needed to make their statements definitive to highlight their difference from other approaches.

For me that means to again restate the opening paragraph of the first chapter:

What is an eating disorder? It is a defence mechanism of the body that has gone horribly wrong.

I only came upon this belief through a sequence of apparently random and accidental clues. Firstly there was my own experience – if there had been any external resources I might never have had to look so deeply and honestly into myself. Instead, with the benefits of conventional wisdom, I might have somehow gained a part-recovery, a way of living with some of the answer, enough to achieve minimal nourishment but not much more. This would be 'compromising' with the disorder, 'living' with it, not putting it fully in the past.

An example of the lack of clarity in understanding a disorder appears in the New Optimum Nutrition Bible (Holford, 2004). 'In the 1970s, a number of researchers noticed that the symptoms of anorexia were similar in some respects to those of zinc deficiency, giving first to a hypothesis that zinc supplementation might be useful in treating anorexia and possibly also bulimia. During the 1980s and 1990s a number of small trials were carried out to supplement zinc for patients with anorexia as they started to eat and gain weight.

'There were some positive results, with improvements in weight gain, mood, emotional state and menstrual function. The researchers concluded that individuals with anorexia and bulimia may have zinc deficiency. However the complexity of treating eating disorders clearly indicates that while zinc deficiency may be a contributing factor in the conditions, it is neither the whole story nor the root cause' (Holford, 2004, p. 140). I believe the author is wise in not trying to make a case for an eating disorder being a deficiency that can be cured with tablet supplements, yet it also highlights a lack of what *it is*.

The most common uninformed belief is that anorexia and bulimia are attention getters. That if the person wished to they could start eating normally again. I recall one client who finally found the courage to reveal to his mother that he had an eating disorder. Her response was sympathetic listening, followed by 'And now I'd like you to come and eat a nourishing meal with us'.

Faced with the baffling nature of the illness, and the grief it causes, practitioners have long been trying to raise the success rate for recovery. With a mortality rate of 10% or higher, and the observed fragility even in recovery, a wealth of possibilities have been proposed.

Minuchin (1978, p. 83) notes 'all therapeutic processes challenge reality as a prerequisite for change. The psychodynamic therapist postulates an expanded self. He teaches the patient that her psychological life is larger than her conscious experience, and helps her to recognize and accept the repressed parts of her reality. The behavioural therapist's relativistic concept sees the patient's reality as a mediated response to context. If the physical and social content changes so that different behaviours are rewarded, the patient's reality will change. The family therapist sees the patient's reality as a highly complex interaction of internal and external inputs.

Change in any significant aspect of the patient's social ecology will in some way affect all the members of the system'.

Treasure et al. (2006, p. 192) writing a more up to date overview of responses note: 'Simple dietary management alone is both unacceptable (in terms of poor adherence as a primary intervention) (Serfaty, 1999) and ineffective as a form of relapse prevention (Pike et al, 2003). Other than this there appears to be little to choose between the different brands of treatment such as Cognitive Behavioural Therapy (CBT), Focal Psychodynamic Therapy (FPT), Cognitive Analytical Therapy (CAT), Interpersonal Therapy or Family Therapy (Hay et al., 2003; Treasure & Schmidt, 2002)'.

Treasure et al. (2006, p. 194) include information from neuroscientific research: 'Evidence from neuropsychology suggests that part of the predisposition to anorexia nervosa lies in the neural template underlying emotional and information processing (Southgate, Tchanturia & Treasure, 2005). It is probable that in part these traits are an innate, inherited vulnerability... the stress response and emotional reactivity and coping which are thought to lie at the core of the development of eating disorders can also be shaped by prenatal and early development experiences'.

Even after recovery, which may only be partial, resulting in an ongoing desperate bargaining with the disorder, there is a sense from both the patient and the professional that exactly what has happened is not fully understood. There can never be a sense of relaxation, of complete confidence that the illness has departed, since its nature may include recurrence. However, once I recovered from my anorexic period it never recurred. And I believe this is because, in looking deeply inside myself, I fully engaged with the true nature of the disorder – and disengaged it. What I mean by this I will enlarge on in the following chapter.

And as I've already said, I completely forgot my anorexic period. Seven years after my anorexic period, still struggling but this time with how to live sanely in an insane society (Apartheid South Africa in the 1980s) I had the great luck to come across an Eastern teaching, which has became the second aspect of my understanding. This teaching was brought to the West from esoteric schools in Afghanistan, Tibet and Nepal (PD Ouspensky 1950).

The single most important piece of information was the idea that rather than there being just 'one body or centre' we have several. The most important of these are our head (the intellectual centre), our emotions (emotional centre), the centre that governs all our movements (moving centre) and the centre responsible for all the parts of us that should remain outside our conscious control (instinctive centre).

I say 'should' because once the disorder gets going it starts to bring these instinctive functions – like breathing and swallowing – into its control, which is why people with disorders sometimes develop elaborate rituals surrounding their digestive and other functions. The disorder is trying to run everything – and it does not have the proper faculties to do so. Since this is part of the reason why the disorder is so disruptive I will elaborate on this aspect later on.

The idea of there being different aspects of ourselves within the larger unit *has* been observed by the psychiatric fraternity. Bion, 'having analysed patients who were schizophrenic, came to the conclusion that even in the mind of the schizophrenic there were areas of functioning which were not psychotic...' (noted by Shipton, ibid, pg 113). And in Anorexia Nervosa and Related Eating Disorders in Childhood and Adolescence, Bentovim notes the 'healthy part and the anorexic part' (Bentovim 2000, p. 349).

Exploring Eating Disorders in Adolescents (2004) is a compilation of essays. I would like to borrow a quote which show aspects of what I understand to be an EDM. 'I didn't want to die but I had to: The Pervasive Refusal Syndrome' by Jeanne Magagna, details the case of Yofang, a young Chinese musician. These are the therapist's notes. Magagna notes three phenomena, of which this is the last.

'Hallucinating a monstrous 'male figure'. This figure functions as a kind of concentration-camp guard. It promises protection to the child as long as the child obeys it by withdrawing from any kind of human contact. When the child attempts to eat, and therefore to depend on the nurturing figures, the hallucinatory male figure threatens punishments. This is the world of the destructive part of the personality against life, hope and dependency. The monstrous hallucinatory figure is at times turned to as a king or 'companion'(p. 136).

I believe that the 'monstrous male figure' is not hallucinated, it is the EDM. But otherwise the aspects of the figure are just as I understand it: something more powerful than the wishes of the individual in which it dwells.

If we accept the idea that the disorder is a defence mechanism that has gone terribly wrong, we can understand why so much of the current treatments are fundamentally incomplete. Medical staff and other concerned parties are unquestionably sincere in their efforts to 'cure' someone with a disorder, but if, which is the basis of my method, they don't understand that the person themselves is *not doing it*, that what they are witnessing is the action of a mechanical body function gone wrong, then surely the treatment is being approached from the wrong angle?

Following from this it's not difficult to understand why professional responses to the manifestations of the EDM have resulted in dissatisfaction on the professional side, and anguish on the patient's side. This is most particularly unfortunate because both the carers and those whose loved ones are affected are clearly desirous of the most benevolent outcome. Unfortunately it must often seem that there is little that can be done if the patient refuses to cooperate. This has led to unfortunate episodes in hospital and residential settings which do not help the overall picture. Lawrence (1984, p. 79-80) details a patient's increasingly traumatic experience of traditional recovery methods.

A situation such as Lawrence details is not far from the experience of women and men I have encountered personally. After I presented a talk about my approach to a group of counsellors and psychotherapists, one of the attendees sent me an email headed 'Finally Someone Who Understands':

'Dear Matthew ... I am mainly emailing you as I have had anorexia myself and came along to the workshop to gain knowledge not only to help others, but ideas on how to help myself. I spent last summer at a recovery unit and have had eating disorders of different sorts for 17 years. The main thing I wanted to say to you is FINALLY SOMEONE WHO REALLY UNDERSTANDS.... I understood all of your theories and how they related so much to me and so many people I have met through the eating disorder support....

'I have been force fed, and it has made the eating disorder stronger, I have been more determined to obey the doctors so I can go home and obey the anorexia....

'To reiterate, your workshop was an inspiration and it gave everyone a lot to think about, it's great that finally the world of force feeding and punishment could be moving on as cures for eating disorders have been stuck in the dark ages for so long. Plug your theories as much as you can it has got to be the way forward, it can't stay like it is.' (personal communication, 2007)

I would also like to mention the experience of a person I met at an eating disorders conference. She had found a way to gain weight on her own, but at one point she had been referred to a therapist by her doctor. She related that in the initial session the psychotherapist had regarded her, silently, for a time, alternatively shaking her head and making 'tssk' noises.

Then she told the person who related the anecdote to me that she 'was too thin to work with. Go and eat three meals a day for two weeks then come back and we'll see what we can do'.

This mode of response to a person clearly in need of immediate help is noted by Em Farrell (1995, ch. 4). 'Extremely primitive feelings are stirred up by anorexics and anorexic bulimics.... Many people wish to feed them up before they will work with them. They do not believe it is possible for individuals to make sense, or perhaps be made sense of, at such a low weight'. McDougall (1989) also notes that even if people are looking for therapy (and in her case she means analysis) they might not be right for the treatment.

However, as my acquaintance put it: 'It's like a doctor saying your arm is broken – come back when it's partially healed and we'll talk!'

Where should we begin to look for the cause of a disorder? One way in which my own work has been positively affected by my coming into contact with analytical theory is in the concept of 'containment'. In fact, I now use the theory to clarify what is necessary in any relationship. Whether friendship or a loving relationship, what both sides needs is that the *other will contain them*. You can also see why a relationship will go wrong – either or both are not contained by the other.

What does containment mean? That the one has an empathic and responsible attitude towards the other, and is able to make sense of what the other cannot. The one trusts that the other will support when they need it. The other also benefits from the containment, in that *they* are contained by the first person's acceptance of what they are doing.

Referring specifically to the early years of baby development, Wilfred Bion writes of 'containment' (1962). That the baby is unable to contain and process its fears so it projects these onto the mother (the containing object). If the mother is able to process these, the baby develops a sense of confidence. However if the mother cannot, these undigested fears return to the child in the form of 'nameless dread'. I have not had a single client who does not respond to the concept of 'nameless dread'.

It is my growing belief, building on this theory, that during the early months the baby develops what I think of as *psychic holes* in its psyche. Just as it takes time for the skull bones to grow and protect the delicate brain, so the process of growth is not only physical but psychic. Nature abhors a vacuum it is said, so rather than contain psychic holes, the psyche's holes need to be filled. So the action of the EDM, once activated, is to fill up these holes with its own destructive manifestations.

Eating disorders are focused predominantly in the category of young (most normally 18) women in the Western world, mainly middle class and white (Lawrence, ibid). But *why* does this apparently senseless, inexplicable and devastating phenomenon occur? In one way, that someone who was sexually abused would seek to punish themselves makes sense – not being able to confront the aggressor, she or he takes it out on the thing closest to hand, themselves.

But why does an apparently happy, apparently healthy young woman, or a young man, or even an older woman or man whose reasons must surely differ, start on a relentless internal battle, using denial, exercise, starvation and vomiting as weapons?

The easiest answer is that often it begins as a good thing.

Once we remember that an eating disorder is a body defence mechanism that has gone horribly wrong, it makes sense that at some point the activation of the defence mechanism was done in a good cause. Before examining this more closely, let's look at another body defence where the cure is often worse than the illness: hay fever.

If you've lain awake at night unable to sleep because your nose is blocked solid, it's cold comfort to realise that your body is actually trying to *protect* you. It is filling your nasal passages with mucus so whatever it is that triggered the response – newly mown grass, blossom, daffodil pollen – cannot enter the system. This makes sense to the body, but since the result is a bleak and sleepless night you might prefer it if your body had not come equipped with such a device. The same is true of the eating disorder mechanism.

There is also relevance in regarding the arrival of Aids in the 1980s. An acquaintance once related to me that a friend of his with swollen glands was taken to hospital. The doctor removed the glands for a biopsy, to determine what was going on. But the swelling of the gland *indicated the body's defence system was attempting to deal with the illness* – by removing the gland the doctor was taking away the body's defence mechanism.

Similarly, in treating eating disorders, by projecting onto the patient external demands, by taking away the individual's self-reliance, we take away their natural ability to cope.

If we as people who have experienced an eating disorder *realised* what it would set off – I will examine the process by which the disorder takes control shortly – then we most probably would have stayed with the presenting problems and tried to muddle through. But we don't. For a while, we think what's happening to us is under our control. We may even, for a time, be deliriously happy.

I remember the first few times I really looked at my body in a full-length mirror. Having been overweight during my childhood, to look at my body and see the outline of bones where previously there had been bulging flesh was obviously very exciting and satisfying. In a way I was answering back all those bullies who had picked on me as being weak and defenceless – no I wasn't a lump of lard, or (my nickname) Roly Poly. *I was totally in control.*

But this is where – given the right circumstances – a disorder mechanism (EDM) unbidden by us wakes up and starts to take over our life. What are the 'right' circumstances?

Evidence is showing that – just like with children and adults who are overweight – it's the more sensitive people who are most likely to develop a disorder (Lawrence ibid). Whether it's because there is an unspoken or overt set of high expectations the individual feels they cannot meet, or whether the child has been coddled or neglected, it's more likely the adolescent who turns *inwards* who may develop a disorder.

Because we've touched on the idea of *inwards* this is a good time to answer the question: why *predominantly women?* There are books that view eating disorders as being a *feminist issue.* (Richards et al, 2001). Orbach and other feminist writers have also focused on the 'personal is political' – and it's women whose bodies are viewed as social property (Orbach, 1980). I have no argument with anyone wanting to claim the political aspect of the illness but I would say that, since 1 in 10 who develop an eating disorder are *men*, to exclude men from the equation is almost like saying the world is only heterosexual (1 in 10 being the most frequently quoted statistic of heterosexual to homosexual).

Here it's also worth noting Shipton (ibid, p.107) 'Gender and sexuality appear to be significant factors, with approximately 20 per cent of men with eating disorders identifying themselves as gay, double the estimated proportion of gay men in the population'.

What is to me more interesting is to understand why *some people turn inward.* And that is more to do with the individual's sensitivities than their gender or sexual orientation. The fact that more women develop disorders than men, the fact that the most common age is 18, to me means its predominantly about that time when both sexes move from *childhood* to *adulthood* that's the real definer (and later in life, it's trying to hold on to a specific period of life and not getting 'older' that can set off the mechanism).

Since boys and girls are encouraged to develop in different ways, with boys favouring an outwards orientation, since its more acceptable for girls to talk for hours about their internal lives, it follows that adolescent girls will be more likely than adolescent boys to be susceptible. Additionally boys who see the heterosexual world around them and sense it is not for them, on the other hand, also often instinctively turn inward, to find a safe space. Yet we should also try to understand who are the other 80% of males affected who are heterosexual.

It is this turning inward, this looking inside to a private world in which control can be established – often fleeing a too-cruel world, or one that just doesn't understand – that needs to be present in the triggering of a full-blown disorder.

Here I make a distinction between sub-manifestations or temporary situations in which someone loses weight and a more chronic condition. Individuals report, for example, that when they are severely stressed they 'lose their appetite'. This may be defined as an EDNOS – Eating Disorder Not Otherwise Specified – but since the persons report that when the stress alleviates they regain their appetite it is clear that it does not involve a full-blown eating disorder.

So, just as a migraine needs a variety of triggers – tiredness, back problems, allergy to food like chocolate, cheese and wine – to kick in, so a variety of causes need to be in place: a *disordered environment.*

Faced with the relentless breaking down of traditional values – family, government, social interaction - and the rise of a babble of confusing, frightening media and news coverage (pictures of war atrocities and widespread famine) – obviously the sensitive individual may find it all too much.

Plus there are the relentless demands of the advertising-fed media favouring the thin body over the normal. And this is without the percentage of people whose history involves sexual or physical abuse. Basically, just living with your ears and eyes open is enough to overwhelm.

And then there is the element of 'nameless dread'. An upbringing in which – often despite the most caring and concerned parental input - there was not the right containment may possibly continue not to provide the essential psychic food for the developing child. For a while this may be a hidden or only a potential threat, but with the change from adolescence to adult new instinctive skills are expected to have been internalised and integrated. Without these the adolescent feels exposed and inadequate for the more complex intrapersonal, interpersonal and specifically sexual and emotional demands being made by their age and situation.

And here the growing number of children affected needs to be included – it does not take puberty for a disorder to manifest. It is also important to state here that exploring eating disorders is not about finding the right words with which to blame the parents. No one provides a psychic map for raising children. All we can do is work with the facts and leave the blame outside.

For me, it was the comfort of realising that by focusing on my ongoing series of goals – 'I'll lose another five pounds – no, ten' – I didn't have to face the problems of knowing I didn't know *how* to be an adult. Having hidden and denied my other needs by being overweight, I didn't have whatever confidence was necessary to let go of childhood and move on. Instead I became obsessed with my internal world which offered a sense of comfort similar to that I had found in food-as-compensation.

For others it's the way the disorder steps in to stop them agonising about some situation in their life. As you will go on to read, the female anorexic client I describe developed her disorder as a result of the impending death of a much-loved relative. In order to 'freeze time' the disorder stepped in. And once her uncle had died, she continued to allow the disorder to 'protect' her from the pain of what had taken place.

This is what I call 'the anorexic Promise'. My work so far has shown me that everyone's disorder has a Promise. Generally this

Promise boils down to the disorder saying that in exchange for you giving it your life energy, it will save you from pain.

And let's face it, wouldn't we all like a pain-free life? As Hamlet asks 'Who would bear the whips and scorns of time, the oppressor's wrong...' – when the disorder can take care of life's problems for us? Of course this question is only rhetorical. If the disorder *wasn't* a disorder it could be a proper help. But being a *mechanism* it just doesn't know when to stop, when enough is enough.

How does the cause behind anorexia differ for someone who will go on to develop bulimia? A client I've worked with has labelled it as coming from his sense of masochism, and he stated that he identified with Freud's concept of the narcissistic self. My experience of him was that he was often unusually hard on himself – something that therapists will often note in clients or patients. When asked *why* the person needs to be so hard on themselves there is often no clear answer. So to me that is 'EDM thinking'.

Some years ago I read that anorexia is all about a desire to achieve independence, and bulimia is all about punishment. When I discussed this with a prominent TV therapist she said she didn't think it was possible to have such a neat definition since in her experience both illnesses may have both of these characteristics present. Since we are working with a psychic illness, it seems to go beyond and outside easy definitions.

From observation I also believe a *skewed sense of responsibility and a propensity towards guilt* is involved. Externally there is a difference in the action of the eating disorder mechanism (EDM): rather than denial and starvation, it's binge and purge. Both are being driven by the mechanical acting-out of the EDM.

Wilfred Bion, writing about the process of learning through experience, (Bion 1962, p. 11), notes that 'the need for love, understanding and mental development is now deflected, since it cannot be satisfied, into the search for material comforts. Since the desires for material comforts are reinforced the craving for love remains unsatisfied and turns into overweening and misdirected greed'. This is pertinent when trying to understand the bulimic's unsatisfied and probably unacknowledged craving for sustenance. Greed in the form of food is symbolic of a spiritual and emotional hunger that cannot be satisfied through eating.

This is why, using the information available to them, analytical psychotherapists and analysts have focused on the idea of the cure for an eating disorder being to *repair the gaps in previously experienced relationships*.

This is clearly relevant and helpful. But it does imply that the causes of the disorder are entirely emotional and according to my experience and work with clients this makes for an incomplete understanding. In the cause of greater understanding I suggest that *it's the EDM that causes the food to be rejected*. It is not that my approach differs from the therapeutic aims of others, only that I am suggesting an actual *physical/psychic component* – the EDM – which needs also to be factored in.

Anyone interested in eating disorders can read up on the general theory of cause in any number of other books. I am more interested in focusing on the causes that I have encountered *personally* since in this way I can also illustrate the evidence for my theoretical approach.

Most comment on the cause comes from the psycho-analytic and medical worlds. Since my degree is in Rogerian therapy (for Carl Rogers, creator of the client-centred, humanistic approach) my observations will be in any case different in emphasis (Rogers, 1954 etc). So, when drawing on the sources for the basis for my theories – personal experience, Eastern wisdom – I must add the third aspect - Client-Centred therapy.

When I decided to train as a therapist I looked at various approaches: Gestalt, TA (Transactional Analysis), CBT (Cognitive Behavioural Therapy). I chose Client-Centred Therapy because the emphasis was on *being,* not *doing.* I liked that Client-Centred Therapy recognised the necessity of the *client* being in control rather than the therapist, that the emphasis is on the client's understanding. It is the client who needs to live in the world outside, therefore it stands to reason that reinforcing and developing the client's ability to function outside the session was most important. Rather than breaking down, building up.

It is widely understood that the illness *does* function as some kind of 'holding strategy'. Most often when people arrive in therapy they have been supporting themselves as well as they can. That, however, has caused them additional problems. With eating disorders the illness has become a crutch, or a tool with which to face the world. Turning inward, focusing the day around the time when one can be alone to manifest the disorder becomes a genuine coping strategy.

The whole rationale of the EDM is that it cuts off the pain of the outside world. And it's this aspect that has led me to understand that the EDM is a *defence mechanism* rather than a malevolent foreign body lodged within like a monster from science fiction.

There are of course, many causes of the initiation of the EDM. In my case, as I got happier and happier as the sliding weight reduction indicated control and an end to body shame, there came a natural point at which my body, beginning to be starved, would naturally have lost the will to continue the process of losing weight. *This is when, in my understanding, the EDM fully kicks in.* I explore this crucial phenomenon shortly.

Some of the literature emphasises the sense of unhappiness, of lack or emotional neglect in the family. Bruch, writing in Eating Disorders. Obesity, anorexia nervosa and the person within (1974, p.79) notes: 'Asperger speaks of the mothers as unable to provide the necessary warmth and security because they themselves were neurotic. The fathers were described as soft, inactive and unable to take a stand against their wives. To Asperger these traits (i.e. eating disorder) are manifestations of a constitutional psychopathology which is handed down from mother to child, and does not indicate a psychological origin of the illness. Gruen and Feldeman-Toldance felt these children suffered from 'severe love deprivation', that the parents lived in loveless marriages that did not satisfy either of them'.

This sense of emotional deprivation rings true for myself – but a recently joining client just wouldn't buy it. He said that he had no memories of neglect, could not identify a particular time or situation – yet in late adolescence he had started to have a problem with food. He said: 'for me it was an attempt to get something right. I might make a failure in other aspects of my life, but controlling my food is something I can do successfully'.

To him there was no 'loveless marriage', no 'psychopathology handed down from mother to child'.

Therefore, to adopt an approach which, in the case of analysis, seeks to repair the holes in former relationships by creating a completely solid and dependable relationship with the analyst, working with this client would not be as effective as the manner in which we chose. This client said: 'I want to work on how I am now. I want to be able to widen my food intake and not be pre-occupied with maintaining the awareness inside me (ie the EDM) of something that prevents me'.

If the emphasis on cause is not on the idea of neglect, it can also be on the opposite, an over-abundance. Bruch (1974, p. 107) quotes: 'In those days again, it was lack of food that drove fainting bodies to death; now contrariwise it is the abundance that overwhelms them'. This was written originally by Lucretius, (96? - 55 BC) and proves that there really is nothing new under the sun. And of course her title, The Golden Cage, reinforces the idea of *abundance* being the culprit.

In Exploring Feeding Difficulties in Children (2004), Lynda Miller writes about Jenny and her baby, Anna. Kleinian theory posits the idea of the good breast being that which is available to the baby, and the bad breast being those times when it is not. Miller makes the point that offering the 'good breast' as an answer to all the baby's needs does not make for success. 'The popular term 'demand feeding' is not truly applicable here, as Jenny would offer Anna the breast whenever she showed any sign of distress, even when a feed did not seem at all to be what the baby had in mind' (p. 2). 'The breast' as Miller notes, is not 'a remedy for all discontents'.

Without my wanting to turn this book into a recap of analytical theory, the writing is so rich and informative that in this 'cause' chapter I must include some references. In Theatres of the Body (1989), McDougall notes (p.45): 'The image of the internal mother becomes extremely dangerous. When there is no fantasy of the father's penis playing a libidinally and narcissistically enhancing role in the mother's life, the mental presentation of the mother's sex (which she transmits to her child) becomes that of a limitless void'.

Also, in On Rejection, Adolescent Girls and Anorexia (1997), Likierman writes (p. 65) of one mother-child dyad: 'she was … using her daughter as a container for some of her own unprocessed emotions. These unprocessed emotions amounted to an inchoate mixture of mother's neediness, both infantile and sexual. However, there was another crucial element in this tangle. As well as demanding containment for herself, mother was seen as unable or reluctant to offer it in return. She was experienced as failing to contain her daughter's infantile emotions and needs.

'The mother-daughter relationship fluctuated between an over-closeness in which my patient experienced herself as the recipient of inappropriate projections, and long periods of detachment in which my patient felt abandoned to process her own needy infantile states'.

This expands on Bion's concept of 'containment' to illustrate how this cause may later manifest as an awakened EDM. Because – as I am exploring with my clients – it would appear that by not being able to process the two needs of dependence and independence (as explored by Klein) a developing baby may, as I have already mentioned, develop holes in their psyche.

These psychic holes may be worked around for some time, but at the stage when the gaps become too noticeable, these holes are filled by the actions of the awakening EDM.

What this means is that there is a direct causal relationship between the unhealed holes in the developing infant and the necessity for the EDM to awaken. This is, again, why I see it as a defence mechanism: it provides in its own way what was not instilled in the developing child by a combination of internal and external processes.

In its simplest description, psychic holes are carried around within the individual as a result (from a number of different causes) of their earlier life. Without the full psychic armour needed to cope with the world, the EDM wakes up and takes much of the individual's energy to do its work. The longer this goes on, the more completely the EDM can be expected to have infected and infested all parts – intellectual, emotional, moving and instinctive.

Marilyn Lawrence writes in The Anorexic Experience (1984, p.51): 'We might say then that anorexia often occurs as a response to a crisis about autonomy and independence. Women are less likely than men to be able to resolve such conflicts and are therefore more likely to be driven to producing symptoms such as anorexia'.

I am offering the idea that it's a mechanism, the EDM, that wakes up and does the work. Particularly, as I stated a couple of pages ago, that just at the moment where a person would normally be expected to lose the energy to manifest an eating disorder's symptoms, the *EDM becomes fully engaged to continue the process.*

There *are* issues of independence, but I see them in a different way. And of course, the independence of the person with a disorder is entirely false because *internally they are trapped by the EDM.*

Therefore when a person noticeably thin is still rejecting food, or bingeing and vomiting, I am suggesting that the EDM is in control. The EDM, by its nature, wishes to live life in disorder. Since its purpose is to *distract and otherwise engage* the person, then all its crazy manifestations become reasonable and logical.

Bingeing, purging, denial and exercise are all aspects of the manifestation of the EDM. I remember spending hours picking the perfect chocolates at the local Woolworth's sweet counter. After a pound of these I would then down litres of orange juice in the misguided (EDM thinking?) belief that the juice would neutralise the chocolates' sugar.

Every person affected by an eating disorder finds their own bizarre and disordered behaviour. Obsessing about calories is common. I know one person who would sit 'impossibly upright' (as described by a fellow worker) in their office chair so as to burn up as many calories as possible even sitting down. Such behaviour belongs to the illness, an illness of the body, the mind, the emotions and the spirit. Again, because I see these functions of the body as being linked, but separate, it needs to be understood that the illness is in *all the centres*.

To recap, there comes a time when the person does not have the abundance of willpower needed to continue the fasting, exercise, purging regime. *This* is why I emphasise the concept of the EDM. Because it is at this point, when logically the person cannot possibly have the conscious will to continue to reject sustenance, that the EDM entirely kicks in and takes over.

When I first wrote of this theory (Campling 2006, internet site) I believed that the disorder was an 'artificial centre, which robbed the other centres of energy'. I have now come to believe, in observing other aspects of its character, something similar, but different in its location. I now believe the EDM is a function of the *moving centre*.

If we remember that the moving centre is the name given to that function of the body that controls all physical movement, the *observed nature* of both anorexia and bulimia becomes the best evidence. Anorexia involves, broadly, too much and inappropriate exercise, plus a drive to reduce and cut out food. Both these involve a *movement*. Similarly, bulimia involves the movement – a cycle – of bingeing and then vomiting.

I have discussed with a bulimic client how, even when he takes in food without intending to bring it up again, he comes to a point where he realises the food 'can only be ejected'. We looked at the movement of ingesting to rejecting as a cycle, of which ingesting is only the initial phase. This is a *movement*, a cycle which is under the control of the EDM, in its capacity of a defence mechanism rooted in the moving centre.

And *this* is why shouting at the disorder, begging the person to eat, logically arguing etc has little effect. Because your right arm can throw a ball, or catch one. It can pick up a pin or a heavy weight. It can write or turn the page of a book – but you don't ask your right arm to work out a mathematical problem. It *doesn't have the ability*. And neither does the EDM – when the ability needed is the one about getting the person, in a functional and positive way, through the day.

Instead the EDM can only operate with the characteristics open to it – some kind of movement. As my clients have noted to me – 'it doesn't have a *plan*'. Its only plan is to make itself feel secure by manifesting the very narrow set of functions it recognises: exercise, denial, bingeing and purging. This phenomenon has been noted by others – in Women's Secret Disorder, a new Understanding of Bulimia (Dana, Lawrence, 1988), it is noted (p. 148): 'There seems to be no point to it; it doesn't seem to achieve anything'. This understanding that the disorder doesn't have a plan is central to recovery and will be enlarged on in the next chapter.

While I was developing my concept of exactly what an eating disorder is, I thought of the story of The Sorcerer's Apprentice. In the folk tale, you will remember that the apprentice, using the sorcerer's wand, has brought the broomstick to life. He orders it to fetch pails of water to fill a water butt. For a while the apprentice is thrilled to have the broomstick doing his job. But when the butt is full, the broomstick keeps going – then it multiplies – and eventually the whole room is under water. Even though the broomstick is also in danger of drowning it doesn't stop its task – its only function – of filling the butt with water.

And that's what the EDM does – it just continues to deny, control and purge, long after there is any *sense* in it. However there is another side to the EDM – its own sense of terror. It is vital for you to appreciate that the EDM is in a constant state of panic and terror because it changes the perception of how we work with it.

When a person with a disorder is offered a plate of food, it terrifies the EDM. Not because it can rationalise that food won't hurt it, and will in fact allow the 'host' to continue living, but precisely because it *can't* understand. It doesn't have a brain, it's a function of the moving centre. So it can repeat the same gesture till eternity – *but it can't think about what it is doing.* And *that* is exactly why it is so dangerous. It has only one response to the whole of life.

So not only is the person not in control, the *only* response the EDM has is to express itself (and get reassurance) in manifestation. Starving children will sneak out of bed to exercise. Painfully thin adults will drag themselves round the block for a late-night walk. In both cases a temporary satisfaction is gained by the EDM, which, since it is in all the centres, is then experienced by the person themselves as feelings of relief and safety. Please note that there is no contradiction between my saying that the EDM is rooted in the moving centre, but that it is in all the centres. The EDM *seeks to gain control over all the centres*. Since it has 'first dibs' on energy, and since it is the essential nature of each centre to attempt to rob the other centres of energy, so the *influence and control* of the EDM, rooted in the moving centre, spreads and colonises the other centres.

For example, I have wondered about why it is that people with eating disorders *don't feel hungry*. In my own experience I didn't miss eating properly because I had no growling stomach, none of the usual indicators of feeling hungry. I believe that one of the areas where the EDM takes over control is the *sense of hunger*. And since the EDM has a vested interest in not allowing this to be experienced by the person, the sense is simply suppressed.

This description of a 7 year old child comes from Exploring Feeding Difficulties in Children (Williams et al., 2004, p 119). Much of the seemingly bizarre and illogical behaviour seems to make sense when understood as a *manifestation of the EDM*. 'When Marco was not being sick in the canteen, he would eat virtually nothing. He repeated a series of obsessional rituals, which he tried to conceal .... When finally making up his mind to face his food, he would turn the fork round on the table and cut up the food into tiny pieces. His approach to food seemed to indicate a certain difficulty in taking something in and biting, as if he were faced with having to deal with something toxic'. If we read these words as an example of how the EDM manifests, surely they make logical sense?

A long time ago I realised that it doesn't matter where the truth comes from. What matters is that *it is the truth*. This belief has led me to writing this book. The information comes from five sources. Firstly my own experience of eating disorders. Then Eastern wisdom. Thirdly the person-centred ideas of Carl Rogers. Fourthly psychoanalytic theory. And lastly the ongoing dialogue with clients as we both explore, observe and widen our understanding.

In the next chapter I will reframe a family conversation in the light of the EDM. Understanding that the EDM *is* something specific also helps to precisely define what is otherwise vague and unquantifiable in the term 'disordered eating pattern'. Although this might seem like a polite, non-judgemental piece of PC-speak, it does no favours in getting near to the reality of what is going on. Yet if we can acknowledge – even only as a working hypothesis - that an eating disorder is a specific sub-entity, a body defence mechanism that has gone horribly wrong in its action, it then becomes possible to approach recovery from a different perspective.

CHAPTER FOUR

Recovery

Moss Hart, Broadway playwright and director, writing in his wonderful book Act One, recalls an argument he once had with an educated fellow. The book details Hart's rise from a childhood of great financial deprivation to overnight critical and financial success through writing a Broadway comedy. The debate was on the pronouncing of a particular word: squalor. The other man would have it that the word was pronounced 'squay-lor', whilst Hart favoured 'squah-lor'. Finally Hart won the point by declaring 'when I lived in it - it was squah-lor!' (Hart 1960, p.26)

Although I do not end every discussion about eating disorders with the same kind of argument, as we begin the chapter on recovery I can say – 'when I needed to recover from anorexia – *this is what worked*'.

When my first anorexic client began sessions (I had been in practice for over ten years before this, but I was a therapist for other issues) I found that in order to break through the years of unsuccessful efforts of others, saying 'this is what worked for me' worked well. When my client began she was severely underweight and not so much sat as flopped onto the sofa in my consulting room. To have attempted to explain complicated theory would have overwhelmed her. I have read that anorexics, in particular, need only a little nourishment and that includes intellectual and emotional input- 'just a little food for thought'.

So by default I chose the route which in practice worked best. I had only my own experience to guide me. And after her years of listening to theory and the demands of others, my simply described experiences became for my client a wake-up call.

The first step in my own education as to the wider eating disorders picture was when she explained the events surrounding the inception of the disorder (this you can read about in Chapter 6). I had assumed that, like myself, her anorexia kicked in following attempts to lose weight after an overweight childhood. However the cause of her EDM kicking in was very different to mine. Working in a client-centred way I merely *offered* my experience, trusting that she would be able to take what made sense to her and use it.

I remember also another client who presented at one session in despair. I remember the thought *I can't help here – maybe he needs medical treatment*. And then remembering that this person had spoken specifically about bad experiences in the health care system. He had come to me – was my final answer to send him back to what hadn't worked before?

Instead I dug inside myself and remembered what had worked for me. When I had been facing my own mortal illness, how I had managed to come back.

'You need to separate from the disorder' I said, 'and begin to negotiate with it'.

The image that came to me was of an open, and closed, flower. I showed him my hands, the left one with fingers closed, the right open. 'The right represents the disorder. The left your healthy self'. Then I slowly closed the right and opened the left. 'This is what needs to happen. An exchange. The energy in the disorder needs to be taken back, to flow back into the healthy self that at the moment is a closed bud'.

Understanding that the crux of recovery is this exchange shows how far my method is from current practice. Sensitive observers like Marilyn Lawrence note: 'if we understand anorexia as a problem which has to do with control, and if we see the long-term aims of treatment as enabling the woman to take a proper and reasonable control of her own life, to become an effective agent in her own affairs, then surely any approach which begins by taking away the final vestiges of her attempts to control her life must be at best unhelpful, and at worst, downright dangerous'. (Lawrence, 1984, p.81).

To me, Lawrence is talking here about some of the methods being used in eating disorder recovery. I believe that the focus on weighing is not only humiliating, shameful and frightening for the person, it's also not the best evaluator. To weigh someone as the defining method of determining whether the previous week has been a 'success' or 'failure' from the point of view of putting on weight puts an added pressure on the patient.

My own experience with the way food and weight shifts in the body has shown that there is no simple, guaranteed relationship between food eaten in weight gained. I remember joining the family for a cheese fondue one night – the next morning I weighed myself and was horrified to discover I was five pounds heavier. Now I realise that was only a temporary state but at the time it caused me to drop another stone. Overall it is what lies *underneath*, it is the growing understanding in the individual's psychology that is most important.

I am not de-emphasising weight and forgoing weighing in a trendy attempt to say something different by promoting the opposite of what is convention. I believe the emphasis on weight may be counter-productive because when I was anorexic I was *obsessed* with weight. When I began to recover I stopped weighing myself – because I didn't want the scales to have such an influence over me and my behaviour. Therefore, by emphasising weight and especially insisting that patients be weighed at the start of evaluations, it may be that the profession is feeding the *disorder's* approach. I believe that treating weight gain as a by-product of disengaging from the disorder (and re-growing the healthy self) can be a helpful approach. Any emphasis on weight as being the major indicator of success or failure surely keeps the emphasis within the disorder's orbit.

Also, as one of my clients reported, he had easily been able to put on half a stone 'of crap. That's what the disorder was allowing me to eat – junk.' That's because the EDM, being a 'disorder' and thriving in chaos, approved of high-calorie, easily burned so-called snack food – but detested anything that would have been really useful to the body – pasta, baked potato, rice, or any form of protein. The point here is that, since the disorder *is* a disorder, what it likes is *disordered food*.

It must have been noted by others that every single client or patient with an eating disorder, when asked what food they have eaten, has a standard answer: 'fruit'. As you will read in Chapter 7, my gentle response to my client who answered 'fruit' was 'fruit is good – but it's an addition to 'food', it's a supplement, it's not *food.'*

The BMI (Body Mass Indicator) is the most commonly accepted way of deciding into which category a person falls. The BMI is calculated by dividing one's weight in kilograms by height and metres squared. A BMI of less than 20 is underweight, 20 – 25 is normal, and 30+ is considered overweight. It has gained popularity as a shorthand for clarifying the reality of a situation.

With my clients, on the other hand, the most I will focus on their 'weight' is to offer a visual response to how they are looking. 'You've lost a little …?' or 'you're looking healthier this week – how do you feel?'. In my approach, weight gain is a *by-product* of understanding the nature of the EDM, and what constitutes recovery is a different, practical understanding which works its way, little by little, day by day.

However my approach is not seeking to challenge conventional methods, only to offer an alternative way of approaching the crucial question of 'refeeding'. I am not medically trained and I do not want to appear to be offering advice to those who are.

I began the book by defining an eating disorder (as an EDM) and saying that recovery was effected by separation and negotiation. I would now like to examine the process in detail.

If we remember that the EDM is a *defence of the body* then it makes sense that, just as our emotions calm down once we acknowledge what they are emotional about, once the nature of the EDM is understood, disengagement can follow. Here I don't want to imply that just by understanding what's going on, change is instant – as I said to one client it's like imagining you have inadvertently painted your double-storey house black. Painting it white again will take effort.

The key to making the right effort is *awareness*. One client, in the course of our weekly sessions, told me about a book he was reading called A Gradual Awakening. He had realised, without my having to point it out, that *this* was what my recovery process entailed. A gradual awakening to the reality of what an EDM is, and with that awakening, the method to counteract it.

In my background reading of current academic material I came across several references to the patient not seeming to have a clear motivation as to why they were involved in the manifestations of their disorder – bingeing and purging or exercising and restricting food intake.

Of course, from my understanding 'a clear motivation' is not separating the person from the action of the EDM. I have discussed this elsewhere, so let's look at the central idea of 'not seeming to have a clear motivation'. I believe that key to recovery is understanding that the EDM doesn't *have a plan*.

How could it when as I have already said, it has only one (anorexia) or another (bulimia) response to all of life's complexities?

Thus, since the EDM doesn't have a plan, it's vulnerable to being disengaged. One of the key understandings I have made in the course of working with clients is that *if you are active, it causes the disorder to become passive*. Let us consider why.

Look back at the concept of different body centres – intellectual, emotional, moving or physical and instinctive. Another aspect of the centres is that they *rob each other of energy* (Ouspensky, ibid).

This explains why, for example, if you have an exam to do the following morning, rather than studying (intellectual centre) you worry (negative use of the emotional centre). When you finally settle down you discover you can't study because you're too tired: the emotional centre has robbed the intellectual centre and there's no more energy.

Therefore when the person is able to 'wake up', even for a moment, and take stock of their situation, being *active* causes the

EDM to become *passive*. For one client in particular, discovering that the EDM was less active late at night allowed her to do a certain amount of eating at that time. It also allowed her to think about the EDM and detach – for at least a little while. And over time this strengthened her sense of resolve (ie the healthy hand opening as the disorder hand closed).

However, my approach does not in any way involve *tricking* the disorder. There is enough of that about with not telling patients they are eating high calorie food and other forceful methods. On the contrary I will say to clients '*understand* your disorder. Realise that it is trying to help you live your life – it's just doing it in the wrong way because it doesn't have any other resources'. Although I don't believe in the idea of writing a letter to your disorder, as related to me by another client, I believe absolutely in *communicating* with it.

This is essential because unless you do so, the disorder will become quiet, temporarily – and then jump back, usually viciously because it is feeling frightened and overwhelmed. I will illustrate this with a client's experience. She related that she had been in a recovery unit. She managed to put on weight although she felt distressed. After leaving the unit she returned to her usual exercise routine – and doubled it. She soon took off the weight and returned to a sense of 'normal'. In other words, a physical state where the disorder felt relatively comfortable and safe.

I will discuss in a few paragraphs how to shift this sense of 'normal' in recovery. But for now let's just look at *why* the weight gain wasn't permanent. Obviously, in my approach, because the EDM had not been included. It had been challenged and inadvertently antagonised. But it hadn't been engaged with – so after the enforced feeding the EDM kicked in and the person returned to the EDM's sense of 'normal'.

This sort of experience is often observed by people around the one who has a disorder. This is the 'tyrant' aspect of the disorder, and why the behaviour of the person with the disorder is so upsetting and disappointing to those around them. Having had anorexia, I understand that not only is the disorder extremely powerful and in control, as I already mentioned it's also *extremely frightened*.

This stands to reason. Everyone is out to get it. Everyone not only does not understand that it's actually trying to *help*, they are actively promoting its demise. Can anything alive contemplate its own death passively? No *wonder* – for example after a re-feeding programme – the EDM kicks in, desperate to experience itself and feel security and relief. Bulimic clients report that when they vomit *they feel happy and secure*. Anorexics feel security in exercising their bodies.

To fully appreciate what happens when food enters the anorexic or bulimic body we need to imagine a blank sheet of paper. Imagine now that food is dropped onto it. It discolours the paper, it's heavy, it has a *presence* – and in the person, taking in food also results in an immediate change in their consciousness. Clients report how sensitive their body is to the slightest intake of food. Imagine then how greatly it effects the EDM, to have a full meal spilt onto that clean white sheet of paper.

Of *course* it seeks to bring about either hours of exercise or purging. The EDM's sense of wellbeing is dependent on the clean sheet of paper (its sense of 'normal'). Therefore if we follow this belief, forced feeding causes the EDM to become either deathly frightened, or hysterical with distress. What I am suggesting here is that the experts who deal with children or adolescents don't yet understand that when the child or adolescent then strongly reacts *they are witnessing the response of the EDM*.

In a particular client session, another way of explaining came to me. Imagine the outline of a person, drawn in silhouette – that is the person's, and the EDM's, sense of 'normal' – what I term the EDN – Eating Disorder Normal. This is opposed to a person who does not have a disorder, who would have an NN – Normal Normal. Now add another silhouette a little outside the first. The EDM is happy with the internal silhouette, its EDN. Adding the second layer to it seems wrong, alarming.

The disorder's sense of harmony relies on returning the body to the inner silhouette or EDN. This is why, once patients have returned from hospitals or clinics having been 're-fed', they some-times, often even, take off the added weight. It wasn't *integrated* into the silhouette, so that it became a new EDN.

Therefore the way to work is to *gradually* add food elements so that the disorder stays onboard and adjusts to the gradually devel-oping and expanding sense of 'normal' – although the EDM is still present, the EDN is capable of expanding. This crucial understand-ing came to me when I considered what had happened when I had first taken weight off.

Take for example when I weighed 10 stone. That was the EDN – my Eating Disorder Normal, which was below my original NN – the Normal Normal being the self-and-inner regulating 'normal weight'. Once I got down to 9 stone, the EDN *contracted*. This meant that although, previously, when I had been 10 stone, the EDM and EDN had been okay with that, once I got down to 9 stone, the EDN contracted and then, going even a pound over, was a matter of concern for the EDM. Then when I got down to 8 stone, the EDN again contracted, so again I could not go a pound over the new EDN. Therefore, in recovery, the process is a series of *expansions* of the EDN, until finally the person's NN is reached and maintained.

A key aspect to understanding this is to remember that the person becoming *active* makes the disorder *passive*. If the person is keeping the EDM on board, is negotiating with it, is gradually changing their body shape as they take on a little, and a little more weight, then the disorder will adjust to the new 'EDN normal' just as, when weight was being taken off, it continually re-defined what the normal was in terms of weight loss. Be active – and the disor-der will continue to re-define its idea of normal.

A client reported that he was now managing to eat three meals a day. But it turned out these were all fruit: bananas, apples, cher-ries, raspberries. I reminded him of the tragic case of the Brazilian model who had died after a diet of tomatoes. 'We aren't monkeys – we need other foods to survive'. Instead I suggested he stick with the fruit for breakfast – but add yoghurt and some cereal. Eat fruit for lunch – and add a slice of cheese. Instead of fruit for dinner – a salad. In this way the body gets used to new food in a way it can integrate, rather than splitting into two silhouettes – one accept-able and the other not. However the emphasis is always on *negoti-ating with the EDM* – telling the EDM that you need a little more food in order to get through the day, to work, whatever. And of course, it's not about cramming the body with calories.

Another aspect of recovery is managing the expected reaction from the EDM of taking in food. Expected in that everyone has a reaction to food entering the body, but in a starving body this feel-ing is exaggerated and frightening.

Part of my understanding of the importance of this aspect comes from the experience of the allies, liberating the concentra-tion camps at the end of World War 2. I remembered, from child-hood, reading that when the allies liberated the camps, they were faced with wanting to do their best for the starving survivors. I remember reading that they realised that these desperate people could not be fed full meals because their digestive systems couldn't cope. Instead they fed the survivors 'a handful of peas a day'. And they gradually increased the amount, carefully monitoring the individual's responses.

When I mentioned this anecdote to a friend, he supplied the other half. 'Yes' he said, 'they fed them only a little a day. *Because when they had tried to give them full meals, the people died'.*

In other words, it was not an instinctive understanding on the part of the doctors. It was their observing that the exhausted bodies were unable to absorb a whole meal – that it could prove fatal.

I am not suggesting that the survivors had eating disorders – I am suggesting that the method of insisting that people who are anorexic or bulimic 'eat normally' can be as toxic to them as to the concentration camp survivors. Psychically they are in much the same situation even if they haven't arrived there in the same way. Looked at from this perspective, the statement 'I only work with anorexics if they promise to eat normally' could be the cause of a great deal of unhappiness.

What I say to my clients is: 'Eat a little. Expect that your body will have a reaction. But if it's only a little more than the EDM is used to, the reaction won't be extreme' – the EDM will be more likely to accept it as within a normal range (particularly if accompanied by a sensible amount of exercise to burn off the most pressing sense of discomfort).

Here I must state that writing about exercise and eating disorders is a potential minefield. Traditionally 'bed rest' has been prescribed for severely affected persons in hospital. I am not suggesting exercise in *all* situations, but only where exercise can be appropriate. Because I am not a medically trained professional it is inappropriate for me to comment on hospital procedure.

However, as a general thought, I do think that bearing in mind the *body's reaction* to a surge of food a certain amount of exercise is often helpful in processing the food, and not causing the EDM to become disturbed. For myself, exercising was essential for persuading my EDM to accept a little more food each day. Since it is so important, and also controversial, I return to the question of exercise shortly.

So every day, gradually, build on this tolerance from the EDM. When the body first begins, after a long period of self-induced (and EDM induced) starvation, the energy rush is experienced as 'strange, weird or frightening' (according to a client). Therefore keep the rush contained by only a little more food at a time, gradually re-acclimatising the body (which we must remember has been infested with the EDM in all its centres).

As I have stated previously, what I've just written may appear contradictory. What I stated previously is I believe a disorder is an EDM that is part of the moving centre. Now I appear to be saying the EDM is in all the centres. Both statements are correct because the EDM's *influence* is felt in all centres. Therefore, from what began in the moving centre, the person's *intellectual, emotional* and *instinctive* centres have also been influenced (or infected).

It is quite possible to talk to the disorder. For example, to find out what the 'Promise' is. Once you have found out what the Promise is, you then have a plan. As Lawrence observed, the EDM is 'not clearly motivated'. And if you are active, it makes the EDM passive. So this gives the person a way forward, a way out of the seeming chaos and despair.

The EDM being rooted in the moving centre, it seems that people with eating disorders are always on the go. What works in therapy is to be encouraged to rest. To start to listen to the demands of the body for rest and sleep. It is a great breakthrough when an individual can feel upset and rather than act out, instead go to sleep. As Shakespeare noted in Macbeth 'sleep knits up the ravelled sleeve of care' – going to sleep allows the emotional and instinctive centres to go about their work. Clients always report that when they are able to sleep, they wake up feeling refreshed and with more energy to negotiate with their EDM.

What is also helpful – and what I always say to clients –is that they should make some form of notes. Make a note, date it, and then either put it in a box you will refer to, or even stick it on the wall. I remember – possibly in the absence of having anyone else to talk to – I constantly made notes to myself. 'Sleep' said one –'relax', 'smile', 'be happy' – and all dated. The importance of dating was that when, a couple of weeks later, I had the same realisation again, to see that I had had it a couple of weeks previously gave me a greater sense of *trust in myself.*

And this, again, is crucial. Having been hijacked by their own bodies, the person has almost certainly come to doubt their ability to run their own lives. This is of course part of the Promise – 'since you can't look after yourself, give everything to me and I will do it for you'.

But keeping notes – as simple or complex as works for the individual – puts what Carl Rogers called the *locus (place) of control* back in the hands of the individual with the disorder.

While we're talking about *locus of control* (ie the place or seat of control), let's again bring in the work of Carl Rogers, creator of the person-centred humanistic approach to therapy. Rogers theorised that when we are born we are properly in our *organism* (Rogers 1951). That when we are tired, we cry. Hungry, we whimper. Happy we smile – our external and internal selves have a *high degree of congruence* (i.e. what's going on inside us is available to our conscious awareness and evident in our behaviour and communications).

Exposure to the world, being told to shut up when we cry, being forced to fit into others' needs causes us to move from an *internal locus (or place) of evaluation* into an *external* one. We stop trusting our own emotional responses, we become passive and react the way our mother, father, teacher or peers say we should. And we also move from what we could call our organismic self into an artificial *self-concept* that then attempts to run our lives for us.

Sounds familiar? It appears the EDM isn't the only mechanism our body contains. We've all come across people who only seem to be able to know what they think or feel when someone *else* tells them. It's part of what makes the designer culture so popular – if you're wearing the right clothes, you must be a good – or better a cool - person.

Within an eating disorder context, the self-concept may be the way the person has been trying to get through life, while the EDM is the specific body mechanism that has been activated, in response to a single or multiple cause. Therefore a major part of the recovery process is for the person to regain trust in themselves. Rather than fearing the wilful demands of their body (which I would term the action of the EDM), they discover a growing ability to connect the dots themselves, and begin to feel more confident in managing their lives and energy.

This creates a virtuous, upwardly spiralling circle of what Rogers referred to as 'the actualising tendency' – that given the right environment the person *instinctively* makes choices that enhance and promote their health and wellbeing.

I have already alluded to the positive use of exercise, if it is approached with the right understanding of its usefulness. If we look at how the population generally sees exercise, for many people it's an integral part of their day. Even without an eating disorder, someone who is used to working out will complain about feeling out of sorts if they are denied access to exercise for too long – the body gets used to it.

To deny a body that has got used to working out in some form is like denying a dancer his or her daily regime at the barre. Dancers who give up the daily practise report that their bodies 'seize up'.

Imagine what its like for an anorexic body, not only to have energy in the form of food flooding onto the 'blank sheet of paper' but also to be denied its usual outlet of exercise.

So I will say to a client: 'Expect that after you have eaten your body will crave exercise. Do a certain amount – twenty minutes. *Then rest*'. I will also say: 'At the start of the day, *remember to negotiate*. If you need to bike to town, negotiate with the disorder. Say: 'in order to bike, I need fuel. If I don't get the fuel, I can't bike'.

An image that came to me in this context is to think of a pillow stuffed with feathers. If every day you take out some feathers and you don't replace them, there will come a day when the case is entirely flat. Thus it is with food: we have to put a certain amount of feathers in the form of fuel into the pillow case of our bodies, or one day there will be nothing left to take out.

The EDM listens to this. Incidentally you will note that I didn't talk about food, but about *fuel*. This the EDM also understands. Most of the time it's occupied with burning up the fuel of food, but this can be modified by making the taking in of 'fuel' a pre-requisite of any form of exercise, including gentle exercise like walking.

The important thing is to always keep the EDM informed. Although the eye may be temporarily fooled, the body is immediately aware if too much has been dropped on the clean white sheet of paper. The EDM then responds. And if we remember the story of the Sorcerer's Apprentice, the important thing to remember is that the EDM *has no plan*. It has no plan because it is a function of the moving centre, which by its nature does not have an intellectual function. It is mechanically carrying out its 'task' of looking after the person – in its own idiosyncratic, dangerous way. Therefore *we* can have a plan.

Remembering that a little that works is clearly preferable to a lot that doesn't, I don't insist that my clients 'eat normally'. Instead we talk openly about what they are eating. A feature of eating both for anorexics and bulimics seems to be the sort of food *the EDM* allows.

As I said already, what the EDM likes is 'disordered food'. Clients report snatching handfuls of cereal, or raisins or nuts, on their way out the door. The EDM likes high-sugar foods like choco-late and grapes. Items that while they are clearly some form of food are *not wholesome and sustaining*. I remember buying two bars of nut brittle and asking the vendor if they would help me put on weight. I remember the odd look he gave me (I somewhat resem-bling a walking skeleton) and him saying: 'If you want to put on weight you need to eat potatoes and bread'. Which of course I never would.

Reviewing what I have written you may think there is a contra-diction between my saying that the EDM by its nature does not have an intellectual function, and that it's the EDM 'allowing' food to be eaten, as long as it's in a disordered way. What is the intelli-gence of the EDM?

After much thought and observation I've come to the conclu-sion that the EDM has a brain somewhat like an animal. Take my cat for example. He watches quietly as I shut all the doors. Some-where inside he remembers that when all the doors are shut that he is probably being taken somewhere and he reacts blindly to the fear, attempting to get out before the last door is closed against him. Plus animals can be cunning – a dog will demonstrate a high degree of ingenuity in avoiding a bath. You can't argue with a cat or a dog on the merits of going to the vet or being washed, because their brain doesn't work like that.

So if we think of an EDM as having *an intelligence*, but not one identical to our intellectual function, it helps to define what we're dealing with. I was particularly struck by the words of one of my clients, talking about the anorexic Promise. It wasn't, she explained, so much that it was a voice in her head saying 'give me your energy and I will keep you safe'. It was more a *feeling, a sense* in her body that she could interpret. Knowing this, again when the person with the disorder negotiates with the EDM, feelings and sensations are as important as getting the words right in order not only to commu-nicate with the EDM but also be able to sense when the EDM is unhappy or frightened and needs to be carefully handled.

Finally, if you are a person with a disorder, or if you are work-ing with someone in that situation, you will probably have noticed that the EDM isn't always in exactly the same position. During the day and into the night we move through different stages, sometimes being closer to organismic selves, sometimes being more in our mechanical selves.

The concept of our 'mechanical self' is interesting. It's closely linked to our moving centre, but it is in the *moving part* of all the centres. For example, in movement, it's the automatic walking which takes us from the bus stop to home without our having to consciously direct our feet. In thinking, it's the mechanical responses we make in polite conversation while our brains are elsewhere. It's part of us because it's helpful but the problem is that it doesn't know when to stop. So unless we become aware of ourselves, we will mechanically go through life. Having an eating disorder makes 'waking up' a necessity but this has a beneficial effect in giving us generally a more conscious choice over how we conduct our day's events.

Get to know times of the day when the EDM has less authority. And also be aware that most often, waking up in the morning is the time when the EDM, full of energy from the nights' rest, will be most demanding. The anorexic client I write about in Chapter 6 reported that she was totally unable to prevent the disorder from taking over 'the moment I open my eyes'.

This meant a rigorous exercise routine, then a snatched handful of cereal – if anything – on her way out the door. This was followed by a two-mile walk to work, where the EDM rewarded her with a cup of sugarless black coffee.

Clearly the way to effect recovery in this sort of situation is not to expect the EDM to behave any differently. Clients who allow the EDM to make their decisions acknowledge that the EDM is perfectly happy with the kind of morning routine as outlined above. The solution in recovery is to reverse the order – make *you* active, the disorder passive.

And this is best done with a plan. The plan needs to be organised the previous night, so that in the morning, when you wake up, the disorder doesn't immediately take the initiative. Instead something as simple as a chair left next to the bed on the side you get up serves as a *reminder*. The physical action of having to move the chair wakes up the healthy self. Then it can negotiate.

My client used the gentle, often repeated, simple guidelines of my understanding and recovery plan to gradually increase her weight. As she put on more weight, she had more energy to enjoy life, which added another important aspect to recovery – the bringing in of positive and healthy impressions.

This aspect I will enlarge on in the following chapter – Beyond the Disorder. For the present I want to focus on recovery from bulimia.

The single defining trait of anorexia is withholding- withholding food from the body, withholding contact with the outside world. As I am understanding it, the single defining trait of bulimia is violence. By which I don't mean, necessarily, physical violence. I mean violence towards the self, in thought, word and deed.

In my observation there is more likelihood in bulimia, rather than anorexia, of self-harm in the form of cutting etc. Partly perhaps because a lack of energy makes the energy needed for violence less available. But more essentially, perhaps it's more in the nature of bulimia to be violent towards the self.

It stands to reason that purging the body of food is a violent act. Bulimic clients can express shame for the 'disgusting' or 'really unpleasant' act. Yet they continue it – and possibly take inward a deeper sense of self-disgust and loathing. Does this come from the EDM? Certainly it appears to me that it is the EDM rather than the individual talking.

But regarding the violence of a bulimic, I think it is more that the violence was there *before* the activation of the EDM – the EDM is, if you like, an additional dimension of daily hell. What can be bewildering to the outsider is why *would* someone want to bring up their food? Of course once the EDM takes over the person has no choice since its sense of safety is predicated on its own disordered sense of 'normal'.

But in any case, the person, until psychically healed, would most probably wish to vomit as proof positive of their unacceptable behaviour and self. Therefore in addressing the recovery of a bulimic, the instillation of self-respect and self-love is absolutely vital.

Clearly just telling someone they need to love themselves does not accomplish the desired aim. It more often than not provokes a deeper sense of self-disgust because the person feels unable to accomplish what, when it's voiced, presents as a simple enough task. Bion, in Learning Through Experience, postulated the concept that unless someone had internalised the *ability* to absorb change through exposure to a therapeutic source (having what he called *Alpha Functions*) they would not be able to benefit from outside support.

If, instead, they had what he called Beta Elements, they would be unable to change. It is necessary to note that Bion was referring to work with psychotic patients but there is information here useful in our present focus.

I remember, in the first two years of seeing clients back in the 1990s, gradually realising that some of the people who came for therapy just couldn't make the move from what Rogers called 'a state of incongruence' into a more integrated, congruent way of perceiving their inner and outer lives. One client expressed it thus: 'What you are saying is making sense to me intellectually but I don't have anywhere inside where I can *feel* it'. This is roughly the same understanding Bion was working with.

What I then said to clients who appeared frozen was that they should imagine that inside them was a tuning fork. This fork vibrated and drew impressions towards it – good, positive impressions. In other words, if the client did not already have internalised a method for taking on board the good energy released in our sessions, by thinking of the creation of such a device they might be able to grow the essential part within themselves.

I now propose, particularly for people with bulimia, suggesting very much the same. It can be so taken for granted that the bulimic person will trash themselves verbally (and in other methods) – therefore rather than spending too much time in the session hearing about their self-loathing, propose the concept of the internal tuning fork. Or anything else that makes sense – the basic desire is to overcome beta elements and create alpha functions. And of course, it needn't only be people with bulimia who can gain from this sense of an internal tuning fork.

But for now, as a general rule, rather than making the bulimic feel worse about themselves (as happens when they are faced with the 'failure' of acting out in a bulimic way, as I have heard takes place in some institutions) the bulimic child, adolescent and adult *all* need to be supported as they attempt to feel better about themselves. Shame and accusations merely strengthens the EDM's hold.

This is, again, where Rogers' client-centred theory comes into its own. Three of the six conditions proposed by Rogers are 'empathy', 'counsellor congruence' and 'unconditional positive regard', Such a method of working would have a particularly positive effect on a bulimic client or patient. Unconditional positive regard is not weakly agreeing with any statement the client makes: it is emphasising the *worth* of the client, and underlines the *value* the therapist places in them.

For someone who has been mis-understood, bullied or abused in any way to feel that *merely by being themselves and being human* they are entitled to respect can be a powerful force in opposing their self-defeating and self-deprecating internal conflicts. Specifically, as you will read in Chapter 7, it was my pointing out to my client that he had been able to *contain* a complex emotional situation that caused him to re-evaluate himself and to loosen his self-hatred.

Now that I have outlined my recovery principles, I would like to quote from Menuchin again. Writing in Psychosomatic Families (ibid, p. 3) he details an argument in the hospital between Deborah, a patient, and her mother and father. Menuchin quotes as an example of an enmeshed family dynamic – ie where the dynamic is frozen by the conscious or unconscious words or actions of the family members. He is illustrating the necessity for a family rather than individual approach to recovery.

What I would like to draw your attention to is Deborah's attempts to explain what's going on inside her. She is trying to tell her parents that *she is not in charge* – ie that the EDM is running her life and making her food choices. She is scared of what is inside her and is trying to accommodate its demands. But they are not hearing her:

Deborah: She (a dietician) told me to order what *I* wanted. And she said cottage cheese is a very good source of protein, and I don't have to eat all that –

Mother: You have been losing weight ever since you went on cottage cheese and apples ... Doesn't that mean anything? You have to start to gain. Do you understand what that means? You have to order milk shakes, cakes, pies –

Deborah: I don't want that stuff! I don't want it!

Father: Your life is involved (previously her mother said she might die) and you have to eat .... To me cottage cheese is a side order ... Deb, eat what's on your tray.

Deborah: I don't like this!

Father: But eat it.

Deborah: No! No! I don't care. You can shove it down my throat. I'll get sick and I *will* die.

Mother: Well why don't you order something else then? Another kind of food?

Deborah: Because I ordered cottage cheese! And they said they would give me meals three times a day if I wanted it.

Father: You *have* to eat meat three times a day.

Deborah: No, no, no! You know a growing girl eats what she wants. Oh golly, you *make* me eat it!

Mother: A normal girl eats certain nourishing foods, and then she eats other things that she likes as well. You are starving your body ...

Father: Dr Minuchin said today you can get out of here at 88 pounds.... I know you are going to eat, and you are going to eat well, because if you want to get out of this hospital you are going to eat.

And you are gong to put plenty of weight on. But the thing is this Deborah. You are starting on the wrong foot, and you are acting wrong. I cannot understand the difference in you between last night and this afternoon. Last night you told me 'Dad, I am going to *try*. I am going to eat ....

Deborah: I ate the peas instead of apples ....

Father: But I told you last night that *whatever* anybody gives you is not poison. It is food. It isn't going to hurt you.

Deborah: I can't eat that much! You have to remember that I am –

Mother: Deborah, you don't have to eat that much. But eat food that will help put weight on you.

One can only have sympathy with the frustrated mother and father, faced with their daughter's inexplicable illness. It is particularly poignant that, in terms of my approach, she appears to be instinctively aware of the nature of the EDM, but is unable to communicate this to her parents.

I agree with current practice that there is logic in looking at the whole family rather than only the individual who is manifesting a family dysfunction. However there are plenty of families where there is incomplete communication and not all of these produce an anorexic or bulimic child. Also, there is the phenomenon of the disorder making its appearance in later life. And the example of the client who had nothing to report on her upbringing, she could remember no particular discord (which I have read echoed in the statements of others, as well).

As Buckroyd notes in her introduction to the special issue of Counselling and Psychotherapy Research (2005, p. 187): 'Anorexia has been identified and diagnosable for more than a hundred years, yet we are still at an early stage of knowing how to facilitate recovery. We now have some ideas, some better tested than others, but no more than that. The National Institute for Clinical Excellence (NICE 2004) guidelines recommend CBT for bulimia, but commented that its success rate of 50% indicated that further research into treatments was urgently required'.

Obviously I write this book to offer further research.

Even when a person with a disorder no longer wishes to be locked within its manifestation, they are still enmeshed in the result of the disorder's taking over control of their physical, emotional and mental functioning. What to do to bring about a full recovery is explored in the next chapter.

CHAPTER FIVE

Beyond the Disorder

If you do not and never have had an eating disorder, the idea of looking beyond would seem to be a joyous one. Not being caught up in an exhausting ritual of denial and exercise, or bingeing and purging, would seem a profound relief and also the chance to live a rewarding and happy life.

But people with disorders don't see it like that. What is beyond feels like a terrible void, a spiritual and physical emptiness, more terrifying in concept than any manifestation of the disorder.

Yvonne Round, in her contribution to www.eatingresearch. com, notes: 'When the patient finally 'takes the risk' and reaches the professionals, the carer's worries/role are far from over. The patient has ambivalent feelings about his/her illness.

'Letting go of the illness FEELS like letting go of the only STABLE thing in their life. It's their way of coping. The FEAR of losing this prop and being unable to see a BETTER way is one of the greatest obstacles to be overcome on the rocky road to recovery (Round, 2001).

Writing from personal observation, Round clearly perceives the apparent dichotomy. There are three reasons for this.

Firstly, if you remember that the EDM is in all the centres including the intellectual, it is not the person who attempts to think of life afterwards, *it's the EDM itself*. And of course it can't contemplate what lies beyond its own death. This is why the proliferating 'pro-ana' and 'pro-mia' sites (for anorexia and bulimia) stress that 'living positively anorexic is the best, the only way to live life'. Although it's a person who's written this, the view is that of the EDM.

Secondly, for what may have been a very long time, the person has grown used to allowing the EDM to think their thoughts, make their decisions and take care of their painful emotions. Therefore contemplating beyond the disorder brings home to the person just how naked they are, how empty is their life toolbox.

Thirdly, and following on from above, the original reason the person developed the disorder – the reason why the EDM woke up and started to live the person's life – was because they didn't have a decent set of emotional and mental tools with which to tackle, to quote Hamlet again, 'the slings and arrows of outrageous fortune'.

This is another reason why I emphasise how recovery needs to be a gradual process. Remembering the closed hand that needs to open, the open hand that needs to close, this works best as a flowing, organic motion. Try it. The more slowly you effect the change, the more the whole body stays in touch with what is happening. The quicker the exchange, the more violent the motion feels.

This is where building a relationship with the person, if you are a therapist, or looking outwards rather than inwards if you are someone with a disorder, needs to come in. I have observed with clients that, once we got past the worst few weeks where they were in their greatest need, there begins to come a time when they have started to quieten down, life is beginning to look hopeful again – but then they fear what is to follow. This is the crucial stage where the person can begin to imagine what life without the disorder might be like, but still holds onto the comfort and safety of the EDM.

Clients report that taking in food feels 'weird' and it sets off the desire to either exercise or purge. This is only to be expected – and part of giving the right information is stating this squarely. We all know the effect that heavy food can have, or a bar of chocolate – with someone with an eating disorder the effect is intensified because the starving body has a greater than normal reaction to the energy of food.

As I have said before, it was my experience, and it has often been helpful with my clients, to continue some form of exercise (other than in extreme cases where anyone would see this is unwise), since the resulting energy output is helpful in processing the anticipated pressure from the EDM that results from an increased intake of food.

As much as everyone concerned would wish to avoid hospitalisation and enforced refeeding sometimes this is seen as unavoidable. I would hope that the information in this book may help to avoid matters coming to this point. In other words, that rather than an inevitable descent into a situation where hospitalisation is necessary, understanding the basic nature of the EDM may allow a corner to be turned in recovery before the situation becomes too extreme. However, because this is the difficult reality families and professionals often face, I would like to offer my take on the scenario.

Take a hypothetical case. Let's say Jenny, 15, with a long history of an eating disorder. She has been to psychiatrists, psychologists and analysts and is now in hospital for re-feeding. The nurses are dedicated professionals, and they despair.

They have forbidden her to exercise. They are watchful for signs of bulimia. But she is now so weak she lies motionless in bed while she is fed on a drip. Her face is like a skull and eyes wide with agony stare out anyone who watches her. Nurses have come to avoid her stare. It is felt there is 'nothing more we can do'.

What has made this case extreme, now that we understand the action of the EDM, is not Jenny herself, but the ongoing action of the mechanical EDM. As she has gone to expert after expert the battle between the dedicated professional and the EDM has intensified and Jenny has increasingly become the victim. In fact, by this stage the skeletal face of Jenny can be thought of as *the physical manifestation of the EDM*.

The drip is in fact making her more ill. The new energy entering her body, to the EDM, is nothing less than poison. Inside Jenny a massive conflict is taking place. The EDM is literally being frightened to death.

Recalling the example of the concentration camps at the end of World War 2, by the time the person is in this situation they are not only literally but also *psychically* near death. The EDM, tortured itself beyond its own limits, can think only of 'aborting'.

For professionals this may be a complicated and difficult concept to take on board. The traditional method, guided by the person's BMI, has been to restock the body with food. What I am injecting into this is the idea that the person is *psychologically not capable* of absorbing a great deal of food. Therefore 'little by little', accompanied by an acknowledgement to patients like Jenny that they really are *understood*, is hopefully going to be more relevant to the situation someone like Jenny is faced with.

To return to my own experience. Because I was painfully aware of the delicacy of my internal negotiations, I took great care not to exacerbate the action of the EDM. Instead I did my best to compromise its action but in a way which did not cause it to increase its efforts. For someone like Jenny, I believe that a little that remains within the body is more helpful for recovery than a lot which causes a reaction from the EDM.

I write this knowing how sensitive this issue is, and not wanting to be seen as standing on one side, pontificating because I am not in the position of nurses and doctors faced with a patient in an extreme situation. However, if we remember the learning that came from the concentration camps, it may help to bring about the need for a new approach to refeeding, one that is more in tune with the psychic state of someone with an active EDM.

Although I was not taken to hospital, my body weight would surely have qualified me for hospital. Without the option, I had to be my own doctor and nurse. Fearful of the reaction of the EDM, I used exercise as a bargaining tool. I made my fruit parfaits in the morning – but only after I had walked and swum. Clearly when people are near death, this kind of regime would not be suitable. But often the reason why they are in extremis is because nothing has been done until it is nearly too late. Up till the time when it is no longer helpful, I suggest there are opportunities for exercise to be used as a tool to harmonise the intake of fuel and not cause an over-reaction from the EDM. Remember that for what may be a very long time the person has been used to *something else* handling his or her energy. Once the person is trying to manage that energy themselves, and is increasing their food intake, that energy needs to go somewhere constructive and not become an internal energy pressure cooker.

Hospital nurses, quoted by Lawrence, say they wish they had the willpower of anorexics. Since they don't have the information that in my understanding it's the EDM that's doing the controlling, not the person, they don't appreciate that the person makes no effort at all. It is my belief that the EDM has 'first dibs' on any available energy – so it will use the energy of the food it can't avoid to *work against* the wishes of those professionals involved in recovery.

Therefore, once there is energy in the form of fuel/food, it's vital that it's properly handled. Or the person will continue to be passive while the EDM is active.

Here I would like to quote Warren's 'A Study of Anorexia in Young Girls' (1968). Although obviously recovery methods should have moved on from what is presented here, it is still relevant in underlining the points made above.

'The most gloomy report must be that by W Warren, who described the treatment of twenty children, ages ten to fifteen, who were hospitalised from three to twenty-three months, averaging six months. All patients were kept in bed rest. Other treatments included shock therapy, insulin treatment and tranquilizers.

'Sixteen of the twenty required subsequent hospitalisation for anorexia and other psychiatric disturbances. Eighteen patients were contact at the time of the follow up.

'It was found that eleven of the patients were recovered from anorexia but, of the recovered group, only two were considered psychiatrically normal. One patient had developed schizophrenia, another was leuctomized, two more were considered severe personality disorders, and five others showed "neurotic personality disturbances of varying importance'. Two patients had died, while five had not yet recovered from the anorexia from two to six years after the onset' (p. 135).

After such a devastating role call of failed intervention all that needs highlighting is who these 'patients' were – 'twenty children, aged ten to fifteen…'. What it showed was that *something else* needed to be brought to the process of recovery. As previously noted I offer the theories contained in this book.

On the subject of hospitalisation, in fact in terms of any therapeutic intervention, I would hope that the perspective in this book will help to influence the attitude of the professional towards the patient. Obviously there are many, many sensitive professionals who go to great lengths to assist the patient in their recovery. But sometimes the idea that the patient themselves is just being stubborn, that if they wanted to they could eat (after all there's nothing medically wrong) may make recovery a battle of wills.

I would hope that the concept that the person is not in charge, the EDM is, will change the focus from attempting to force food into an understanding that the patient *can help*. They can help by having the space and the knowledge from the professional to make their own connection with the EDM, and to begin the process of separation and negotiation. Where a strict regimen, with notes drawn up of success and failure, has been thought the way forward, instead gentleness and *trust in the patient's small healthy part* may accomplish more. Confronting the illness, like confronting a mad dog, can of course have little success. Even if the dog is tamed, it may still hate, be frightened rather than reconciled to you and will continue to look for ways to manifest its own nature. But soothing talk and gentle understanding may accomplish what grim determination cannot.

And of course, seeing the patient not as someone deliberately perverse, but someone who is in the grip of something bigger than them, shows the proper perspective in terms of how the professional will regard the person with an eating disorder. They are not themselves. But they can be reached, and cared for, as the information, given gently and appropriately, helps them to detach from the EDM.

When we consider the type of person likely to develop a disorder, we become aware of certain characteristics. Often there is a great deal of energy, energy of feeling in particular, but the EDM has misappropriated this. So once the person is starting to get to grips with the action of becoming active, making the disorder passive, this is the right time to put on the agenda what they are going to do with the energy that is beginning to be felt through their body.

One client of mine decided to do a distance learning course in English Literature, another to do an MA. Studying, getting and maintaining a job (see Chapter 7.), looking for a partner – all these activities are positive and particularly supportive of recovery because *they do not involve the disorder.*

Any and every sort of pursuit the recovering person finds interesting, inspiring or useful can become a great help in the actual process. I remember being told, by a mystic and scholar, that there are *three* types of food. The first is the physical food that we take in. The second is the food of air, which not only keeps us alive, it contains nutrients (which may be why children living in polluted or deprived environments look so pale). The third is the *food of impressions.* I was also told that, as you are already aware, we can live several days without food, a few minutes without air – but we cannot live for a single second without impressions (this is, of course, not scientifically proven. But it is interesting because it is one explanation for the need for the constant voice track in our head – you know, the one that has judgements and little bursts of song or whatever – it's keeping our need for impressions going when all else fails).

This food of impressions is also an invaluable aid in recovery from the action of the EDM and beyond. When I wrote little notes to myself – eat, sleep, breathe, relax, enjoy – each of these was a positive impression. Something that resonated inside me. Something that helped the weak healthy self to grow stronger.

I described this to a client and the next week she came back having pondered the thought deeply. 'Now I feel I have permission to stop being so hard on myself. When I feel that gap, that void inside which I always filled with thoughts of loathing, now I am trying to compliment myself – just little things, like I *do* care about other people and I wish nobody had to go through what I've been through'.

However much energy each of us has, even the truly supersonic, the Branson's and Thatcher's of the world, we all have only

100%. If, when the person hits rock bottom and acknowledges they are ill, the EDM controls 90% of the person's energy, then *10%* still remains in the healthy self. The food of impressions, since it nourishes the healthy part, changes this percentage. As the percentage of energy in the healthy self grows then the percentage of energy in the disorder naturally shrinks. This is illustrated in the action of the closing and opening hands.

And in practical terms, to return to the image of a mad dog, this is how recovery in my approach is effected. Imagine that you are in a room with such a mad dog – something the size of a Great Dane. The salivating Great Dane is your disorder. Obviously you need to be extremely wary of it, you need to obey it, sometimes in the way old enemies do you may even come to temporary compromises with it – but you never stop being afraid of it.

As you take energy back into the healthy self, and as positive impressions grow, the mad dog gets smaller. By the time it is the size of a Chihuahua it can drool and snap all it likes, it no longer has the power to terrorise. (And we are working for it to just cease to operate at all.)

So having something constructive to do with the energy, as it is being released, not only aids the process of positive impressions. It also answers the question: 'What lies beyond the disorder?' One client I worked with was able to make great strides in understanding (and shrinking the Great Dane) because he had a major work project that simply took most of his energy. He just didn't have the energy left over for the traditional two hour nightly swimming sessions. Although he was aware of the EDM pricking inside, it lacked the necessary percentage of control to be able to force him to exercise.

Another aspect of what lies beyond recovery is *symbolic* repair and growth. A client spelled particularly poorly and had little grasp of grammar. (You might think I am being snobbish or elitist here – but let me add that I also had a poor grasp of spelling – before I began to concentrate on it). I encouraged this client to look at her spelling as one way of becoming more *aware*. As she took a new interest in her spelling and grammar not only did she discover a new hobby that took energy away from the EDM, she found a way of 'waking up' in that when she wrote she also became aware of the sneaking voice of the EDM – and would stop to talk and reassure it: 'It's all right. I'm just working. And when I'm finished, because I need more fuel, I'm going to have something to eat'.

That movement of 'waking up' is essential, particularly in the early stages of moving away from the action of the EDM. Remembering that if we are active, it makes the disorder passive, 'waking up' is that moment when we become active. Clients report that waking up, particularly at the beginning, is uncomfortable, frightening, overwhelming. But as they gain more confidence in their healthy self's ability to run their lives, waking up becomes exciting and stimulating.

Clients have reported that one reason it's been impossible to get free of the disorder is that, when they contemplate the time and energy they have *already* spent on it, they become so overwhelmed by bad feelings, or the pain of having felt so isolated and misunderstood, that the EDM comes flooding back to relieve them of their pain. Which of course starts the EDM cycle again.

So a moment of 'waking up' needs to be handled carefully. Again, formulate a simple plan.

In the recovery process you, or your client, will come to a *plateau* where the most immediate painful manifestations have become manageable – but the disorder is still engaged.

Paulette, the daughter of someone I corresponded with on the internet, has an eating disorder but seemed to be 'recovering'. Unfortunately Paulette was caught up in a road accident and taken to hospital. The EDM *immediately* rushed in – and she refused to eat in the ward. This, of course, makes no sense to the outside world, and the hospital staff became quite antagonistic. But when we consider that the EDM has *no other* response, no other behaviour possible other than to deny the intake of food, it makes perfect sense.

What it showed was that there's no easy way out. Paulette's mother had to accept that she had *not* recovered, that all that had occurred was a temporary cessation of open hostility from the disorder. And at the first traumatic incident it stepped in and took over again. The understanding here was that there can be no such thing as a positive compromise with the EDM – only work that will lead to a permanent dis-engagement is worth doing, because otherwise, under stress, the nature of the EDM will again manifest. As I have said to clients: 'Rust never sleeps'.

It's also necessary to emphasise the 'first dibs' situation pertaining to the disorder. As I have already stated, it grabs whatever energy is available. This is crucial for understanding why it is that even exhausted people still drag their way through an exercise routine. And it's why the person doesn't have to think about engaging the EDM when they are under stress. Because the connection is already made, it has passed from the intellectual into the instinctive and moving centres and will happen automatically. That's why it needs to be actively dis-engaged.

Please note here also that when I talk of exercise as *part* of some recoveries, it is only *in combination with increased food/fuel*. I need to emphasise that I do not advocate exercise *only* as a recovery tool. It is a bargaining chip which may be helpful *in some situations*, as it was for me.

On this, I find it interesting to remember and report that about 10 months after I would say I had 'recovered' in the form of disengaging the EDM, I went through a deeply traumatic personal event which took place over several months. At no time did the EDM kick in – I just didn't think of it, and it didn't do it automatically. Which means that a proper and permanent disengagement is entirely possible and this is what my clients work towards.

As the recovery process continues, another visitor you should expect – as in forewarned is forearmed – is the manifestation of other controlling devices. A bulimic client, one session, shared that he had been having thoughts of self-harming. I didn't over-react to this, which would have placed an inappropriate emphasis on what was still only a thought. A thought which had arisen from some aspect of his personality.

Understanding that this thought of self-harming was merely another internal voice, that it may have had little energy behind it, enabled us to talk freely and openly about why my client might want to self-harm. He said it was because he thought he might get the same sense of relief from self-harming that he had become used to from the bulimic cycle.

Identifying the feeling then allowed him to acknowledge that he didn't want to go back to the old habit of self-harming either, that he didn't want to exchange one distressing manifestation for another. It was only in that single session that particular voice was strong enough to make itself vocal, although obviously for yourself, or your client, you would still need to maintain an awareness of whether such a thought was still around.

Using pain to control is much like using addictions. Over the years, my understanding of an addiction has matured into a belief that it's all about energies. In an addiction the usual division of energy – so much for working, so much for pleasure, doesn't hold firm. Instead the pleasure principle (Freud 1920) wishes to take over completely. Since centres steal energy from each other, in the addictive personality the person has so much energy for the addictive outlet – food, drugs, sex, alcohol, gambling, shopping etc – that any sense of perspective is over-ridden by the force of energy behind the addictive behaviour.

Someone who is in recovery from a food, exercise or purging addiction may realise that some *other* addiction is being tested for interest by the disorder. Rather than a proper disengagement of the EDM, the energy that has been used to gathering in strength in the moving centre merely shifts somewhere else – for example into the sex-energy centre (according to eastern philosophic wisdom, the sex-energy centre is rooted in the reproductive organs and is the fifth of the seven centres. The final two are the higher intellectual centre, and the higher emotional, which are engaged at moments either unconsciously or in the case of 'higher beings', consiously).

A person recovering from a food disorder may suddenly find that not only are they amazed and delighted to be alive, but that they have to find a partner *right now*. What had manifested as an internal battle with food and the body then becomes an external conquest to find a partner, or just bed as many partners as possible.

In other words, the disorder mechanism is still active in that just as formerly the disorder's Promise was: 'Give me all your energy and I will make you safe', now the sex centre is saying: 'Give me your energy and I will find you the perfect mate to make you happy'.

It is acknowledged in Alcoholics Anonymous and other 12-step fellowships that people in recovery can become addicted even to the recovery process. Basically as Pandora discovered, once the box is opened, the contents that are released won't just politely go back in. For better or worse, the person who has been through an eating disorder and is recovering in the way I have laid out will also need to find a constructive outlet for the energy now again available to them.

This has benefits. I've noticed that someone recovering from a life-threatening food disorder not only lives life, they embrace it and treasure it. Whereas people who have never 'woken up' may go through life hoping for the best, people who have had to look so deeply into themselves have much more 'can do' about them.

Specifically with recovery from bulimia, it is important to offer a way of living in which self-violence just doesn't figure. Because, like fetching a screwdriver to hammer a nail into the wall, the need and the tool chosen are no longer connected. One client used to torture himself by not being able to take a simple job because part of his internal conflict was to do with the desire to live 'a life less ordinary'. However his illness stopped him from taking even a modest position.

Part of the hallmark of his recovery was his realising that in fact just keeping down a modest job was in itself a much greater task than the overblown fantasies which always resulted in him doing absolutely nothing. Once he was able to let go of the paralysing grandiosity of his distorted vision, he was grateful, happy and fulfilled by the simple job he found for himself – and kept. This was additionally helpful from the point of view of recovering from his disorder because it was ordered so it was beyond the remit of the EDM. In terms of the internal tuning fork, the vibration sounded louder than the voice of the disorder. However he still had to work on negotiating with the EDM as he gradually decreased its hold.

One of my favourite quotes comes from The Gnostic Gospels (Pagels 1980). The author sites one of Christ's 'unofficial' teachings as being: 'if you bring out what is inside you, what is inside you will save you. If you don't bring out what is inside you, what you do not bring out will destroy you'. In the present context, that means bringing out our sense of survival, our sense of joy in being alive, our sense that rather than having to turn helplessly inward we can, with strength, turn outward and make something of ourselves in the world – even if that's only getting through another day with some sort of serenity and self-respect.

This is, I realise, why when things got bad for me I didn't revert to the EDM. Because by then I had tasted the reality of life and I didn't want to return to the dark days of living life as an 'angel'. What I mean by 'angel' will be illustrated in the following chapter.

One aspect of recovery that is often commented on, both by professionals and patients, is the lack of certainty about what will happen next. Often this is expressed as: 'I *think* I'm okay ... but I didn't understand what set it off in the first place, so I can never say I'm sure'.

Henri Rey, writing in Unversals of Psychoanalysis in the Treatment of Psychotic and Borderline States (1994) includes the personal notes of one of his patients, 19 year old Miss R. Rey goes into details of how he interprets her notes, particularly in terms of a pregnancy phantasy (references to the unconscious are written as 'phantasy' rather than fantasy).

Miss R notes (p. 62): 'I still tend to think that my difficulty lies with the means of becoming pregnant rather than with pregnancy itself. But then, the 'fatness' principle crops up, and a pregnant woman's figure is not exactly beautiful, but to my mind, being 'fat' as a result of childbearing is excusable and valid, whereas obesity as a result of gluttony makes me ANGRY, RESENTFUL, HATEFUL OF MYSELF AND OF MY BODY. ONE THING I AM CERTAIN OF AND THAT IS, THAT NO ONE WILL EVER CHANGE MY MIND: I HAVE HAD A DECENT FIGURE FOR A LONG TIME NOW, AND LOOKING AROUND ME, THERE ARE MANY MORE PEOPLE WITH THINNER FIGURES THAN ME. WHY

IS NO FUSS MADE OF THEM? I AM SICK TO DEATH OF BEING FATTENED UP AND OF BEING BRIBED INTO DOING IT. IT IS MY BODY AND I WILL NOT ACCEPT IT AS THIS UNREASONABLE WEIGHT. I HAVE TO BE HAPPY WITH IT AND OF THIS I WILL MAKE SURE.'

This is how the patient's personal notes end. Rey notes in conclusion (p. 74) that: 'The latest news on this brave and intelligent patient is as follows:

It seems that she is reasonably well, but still perhaps somewhat food-and-weight conscious. Her greatest source of pride is being the mother of three children, five, three and one and a half years old. In addition, she is running her own personnel consultancy.'

Clearly Rey has been able to foster a recovery. But looking at the patient's final words – the angry or anguished use of capitals – in my interpretation she is still stuck within what I would term the EDM's frame of reference. This is why I stress the importance of enlarging the EDN – Eating Disorder Normal – so the sense of 'I WILL NOT ACCEPT IT AT THIS UNREASONABLE WEIGHT' – moves into an *expansion* of what is acceptable to the EDM, until finally a maintainable NN – Normal Normal – is arrived at.

My comments on this case should not be construed as unfair-because-one-sided criticism. My intention always is only to take existing material and re-examine it through the prism of the ideas I am developing. To again quote Buckroyd's introduction to the Eating Disorder Special Issue (2005, p.187): 'We now have some ideas, some better tested than others, but no more than that. The NICE guidelines, 2004, recommended CBT for bulimia, but commented that its success rate of 50% indicated that further research into treatments was urgently required'.

I offer all my comment in the light of the need for further research. And in the next two chapters I offer work in progress – case studies of two of my own clients.

CHAPTER SIX

Case Study: Anorexia
'Becoming Your Own Therapist'

You will see that information about the disorder that appears elsewhere in the book is also noted during the chapters on case studies. That is because I made the observations during or subsequent to client sessions. I apologise if this repetition becomes annoying, but since theory and practice, in these chapters, becomes interwoven, to remove the learning as it happened in sessions would greatly lessen the impact of my clients work. In sessions I most often say the same simple things over and over, so that gradually a real, 360 degree understanding is imparted. Therefore I hope that reading the same information more than once will be beneficial rather than irritating. As throughout the book, names and other identifying details have been changed and the story comes from more than one source.

The woman sitting in the chair opposite was well-groomed and dressed. But there was something missing in her presentation. When she turned her head something rounded, the soft fleshy part of the profile, was missing. All of her was sharp, angular, like an Egon Schiele drawing. Sitting opposite me on the comfortable sofa she kept fidgeting from side to side, as though trying to find a position that didn't hurt her vulnerable sitting bones.

'I saw your website. I don't know if you can help me. I have never wanted to seek help. I believe I have to do everything for myself. But I just don't have the strength to keep going anymore. So I'm hoping you will know what to do'.

Of course this was a challenge. If I didn't do or say enough, didn't make a psychological connection, then she might not come for another session – this one had been broken three times before she was able to keep it. Someone with as much information as I had might have been tempted to launch into a detailed analysis of what I took to be her situation, and how I would be able to help her.

But what I was most aware of was her delicacy, her frailty. This was not a case of needing to prove myself: she had already read about my theories. What was needed here was a basic minimum, just enough that she could take in what I was saying safely, not more than she could cope with, verbally or emotionally.

In writing this I recall someone who came to see me, a nearly-qualified therapist, who talked about having felt 'fed up' by the overly dynamic verbal onslaught of someone attached to an eating disorder institution. If she, as a professional, had felt overwhelmed, how might a patient react? I was pleased that right from the beginning of working with Sue I seemed to be in the right psychological space to know instinctively what would help her.

Sue has managed a career in finance. When we first started working together she had just begun a new job working for one of the prominent merchant banking institutions. With gentle delicacy she began to describe her daily routine. She began the day with a step class at a gym near to her office. Then she would have only a piece of fruit before walking to work. She had also walked from work to my house, a distance of more than two miles. She asked for a cup of black coffee with no sugar. In wanting to 'mirror' her demeanour, I reduced my sentences to the bare minimum, and limited gestures and vocal tones. I was trying to match where she was, so that what I did say could be easily absorbed and would not cause her any distress.

In that first session, while Sue was at her most fragile, I concentrated on establishing some sort of rapport and psychological contact. Here it was a great help having had anorexia myself. I talked in a few sentences about my experience. Sue sat, without expression, while my soft words hung in the air around her. When she spoke it was in half-sentences that would fade to nothing.

And yet I was aware that in her daily routine she handled a great deal of pressure, and demands from various quarters. Here clearly was someone who was able to keep going through sheer will – and I was hopeful that that will would now be able to be used for her *benefit*.

At her next session – which she attended without a repetition of the previous cancellations – she described a celebration at the bank. Usually on these occasions she was able to confine her intake to a couple of sips of mineral water. But somehow, seeing the generous array of food, she suddenly felt her willpower evaporate. Although she still attempted to limit the temptation by choosing a small side plate, she filled it several times:

'It was as though there were two voices inside. The one was the usual cry of no! The other said 'go ahead – now that you've started you might as well carry on. Might as well be hung for a sheep as for a lamb.'

Sue at this point mentioned that previous to having anorexia she had been overweight, and said it seemed as though this was an *old* temptation, an old voice spurring her on. This was particularly interesting to me because, as you will see in Section 2, I am coming to believe that overweight may have an OEDM (Overweight Eating Disorder Mechanism) behind it. She reported that she had stayed later than she usually would and had even had the almost unheard of – pudding!

Most significantly, although she had expected to feel dreadful the next day, she woke feeling refreshed even after the high-calorie intake. It appeared that the event was so unusual that *her small healthy self* as it were ring-fenced the calories and absorbed the energy gratefully. However this situation was not repeated in a similar form, so it became an example of how we really *don't* know how our insides operate. Which is why the disorder's way of trying to *control* all these functions is so unhelpful.

In every one of those early sessions with Sue I repeated my mantra for recovery:

'First understand that the disorder is a mechanism in the body. It has taken energy from the proper centres and is trying to live your life. You need to separate from it, then negotiate with it, to gradually increase the amount you can eat.

'Think of it as a flower (I held up my left hand with fingers folded closed, my right hand with fingers spread wide open). What you need to do is (I slowly shut the right hand) close this hand and open this one (the left).'

An important aspect of particularly these early sessions is that I didn't attempt to argue with the voice of the disorder or to try to score points. Rather I tried to give Sue the right voice for responding to the EDM. To hold the idea that it was *trying to help*. Since we saw each other only a couple of times a week at best (her schedule permitting) the focus in the session was helping her to 'become her own therapist'. So when she was aware of the voice or the action of the disorder, she would know more of how to respond to it.

It is very important to be aware of the delicacy of the connection that has been made between the person with anorexia and anyone who is trying to help them. If we remember that even in the session we are being heard both by the person *and the disorder*, then it shows how sensitive we need to be about choosing our words. For the next couple of sessions I was content to let Sue explore her inner world. I did not feel any burden of time. On the contrary she was making her own progress and needed most that the person who heard her had an understanding of what she was going through.

At the next session Sue reported another incident about a celebration. An old friend from college who had been working abroad came home. Expecting just drinks she had been confronted by a buffet. And although, she said, she was hungry, 'there was no way I was able to eat the food. Because of coming here (to sessions) I was able, however, to really appreciate that the voice in my head *wasn't me*'.

I said that this was good, this was a start – for her to be able to *see* that she would have preferred to eat was a sign that she was no longer entirely in the grip of the disorder, and was beginning to recognise the difference between her and it.

Sue talked about the food she did eat. She said that there was a 'food window', usually about an hour after she had exercised in the morning, where she was able to eat. She kept food in plastic containers in her desk and when she started to feel light-headed she would prepare a simple meal. She was aware that the demands for complete accuracy in her job meant that even one overlooked or incorrectly entered digit could be 'disaster', with serious consequences to clients and herself. She was aware that this was an ongoing balancing act, juggling the feeling of light-headedness that she enjoyed with the knowledge that it might make a slip-up more likely.

This acknowledgement by Sue that she *enjoyed* the feeling of light-headedness that is a characteristic of starving is re-echoed by other clients. It is one reason why it is difficult to make a proper psychological connection, because the person is still involved and getting some addictive reward from the action of the behaviour.

With another client I had been able to challenge the situation by saying: 'Yes, you're addicted to the feeling of being light-headed. But what *other* addictions do you have?' He answered: 'My girlfriend' – 'and?' – 'my music' - 'and?'. In other words, by holding up the *one* addictive behaviour and comparing it with a much longer list of more healthy 'addictions', my client was able to get around the perimeters of the EDM and see a wider world.

I also said rather than think of food, think of 'fuel' – the reality is we all need fuel to live. It's not necessary to cram the body with food, or to try and hoodwink the disorder. Gently increasing the food intake, using the energy in a positive way – working, walking, seeing friends – means the disorder will be a lot less likely to panic and over-react.

At this point I still concentrated on simple ideas, gentle pointers. Sue was not strong enough to be bombarded with anyone else's demands including mine, even if I had so wanted. (But of course that's not the 'client-centred' way). We were going at the pace that worked best for her (which *is* client-centred!). I was observing that my concern that she wouldn't be able to intellectually grasp my approach was groundless. As she started to rest more, and eat more, new energy was going to her brain and she was starting to think about things.

When she first arrived she had no sense of where she was. As she began to respond, she started remarking on the pictures and ornaments in my consulting room. At one session she asked me how long it had taken me to recover. I said about six months. This seemed to cheer her, in that it put a guideline on both the disorder and the extra effort of recovery.

And then she needed to go away for a lengthy work commitment.

We didn't meet again for six weeks. When I opened the door, just by looking at her I could tell she was in virtually the same condition she had been when she had originally started working with me. Away from the routine of our sessions she had had only the disorder to listen to. It had begun on her journey. The disorder had told her that the only way to make the long journey safely *was not to eat*. By the time she reached the hotel she was too hungry to talk, and once ensconced the disorder had convinced her that exercise and starvation was the only way she would get through the round of dinners and discussions before her.

We began again at the beginning. Because she was once again exhausted and listless I returned to the simplest of explanations. 'You need to separate from the disorder ... negotiate with it for more fuel ... a little more each day. Remember the open and closed flower ...'.

Then something happened which, although at the time was upsetting and frightening to Sue, was a significant breakthrough. She needed to get home and, with no other taxi in sight, she took an 'illegal minicab'. Only once the car had moved away did she get a good look at the driver and the filthy state of his vehicle. He seemed high on some drug. The man drove along ignoring her directions and request that he stop. She was terrified, frozen. Then something came out of nowhere to save her. At a traffic light, another car bashed into the back of her cab. The driver swore and jumped out to confront the careless driver. Sue took her opportunity, and ran.

Upsetting as this incident had been, I wanted to use it as an opportunity to challenge the disorder.

In the same session Sue had talked about the disorder's Promise. She said the disorder's way of thinking was that only the disorder could give her the confidence to act. Only the disorder could keep her safe and guide her through the day. I referred to the situation with the taxicab: 'The disorder tells you it can keep you safe. But it couldn't. If you had been feeling strong you would have checked out the cab before you got into it. But you were exhausted and didn't see the danger. How did the disorder keep you safe? Wasn't it that the disorder was the *reason* you were exhausted? How can the disorder say that it keeps you safe when it's only answer to all of life's problems is denial and exercise?'

The above, of course, was said in a calm, gentle manner, not accusatory but intending to cut through the clouds of confusion generated by the EDM, and make contact with the part of Sue's mind that was still open to the truth. She was silent and then she nodded. In this session, with the ordeal in the cab, she finally understood that she could not rely on the disorder to look after her. Which meant she had to start looking after herself.

In the next session she reported that she was now having a big salad every night, and listed the ingredients – lettuce, tomato, tuna. The previous night's also included nuts but she still wasn't able to add potato. This was a reference to when she had been in a public place and had wanted to eat potato but she reported that something inside 'felt frightened by the idea'.

She felt she was a long way from three meals a day. She felt panicked at the thought of having something to eat during the day, that she could only eat properly during the 'food window', when the grip of the disorder lessened. At this stage I was still looking for different ways to break into the grip of the disorder. I suggested that she make a *plan*. At the end of the day, when she was most herself, she needed to make a simple plan for the next morning.

The reason for this was that she reported that in the morning she would wake up already in the disorder. So by making a plan the night before, she woke up with a thought of her own. I reminded her that my work with clients was showing me that when we are *active*, it makes the disorder *passive*. Having a plan – exercise for twenty minutes only, then eat something sitting at the table – gave an order to her morning.

That order, of course, was beyond the disorder's jurisdiction. Clients report that the food they are able to eat is eaten chaotically. Of course, I say, it's a disorder's idea of how to eat – disorderly. Therefore when a client is able to eat something in a 'normal' manner, the *impression*, the energy that is released, of the moment is taken into the healthy part of the body, and the energy is taken *from* the disorder.

I also encouraged Sue to consider exercise in a wider context. When someone is anorexic, the relationship to exercise is akin to torture. Although they will drag their aching and exhausted body through a demanding routine they are not doing it for pleasure. However for many people the joy of exercise is a part of their daily routine. It balances out their stress, it keeps them healthy and then there are the benefits of noradrenalin and giving the whole body a good workout.

So rather than suddenly stop exercising, or begin to be ashamed of how much she worked out, the idea was to understand that as her recovery continued she would reach a more natural and balanced relationship between what she ate, and how she exercised or burned up the fuel. Like all therapy, the idea is to achieve a healthy balance rather than begin a different sort of denial. Although the amount of exercise Sue was doing was draining her, her muscles could still benefit from gentle and appropriate exercise, as does everyone else in the normal way.

At the next session Sue introduced a work problem. One of her bosses, an avuncular, older man, had declared to the rest of the office that he was 'going to feed her up'. He insisted she joined him most lunch times and always ordered her food. This was inevitably high-calorie, rich fare that turned her stomach. She quite liked the man as a friend, she didn't want to turn him into a enemy, but she was dreading lunchtimes and had to starve herself for the rest of the day to make up for the food he sat and watched her eat.

I said that his lack of understanding was only to be expected. So much of what is said about eating disorders approaches it from the wrong perception – that the person *could eat* if only someone else says the right thing – that he was just following conventional wisdom. We explored what she could safely say to the man. Finally she decided she would just explain that she had an eating disorder. She told the man that she had come to realise there was something concerning going on inside her and that she was seeking professional help. Fortunately he took this as a compliment to himself, since he believed he had brought this to her attention, and, 'mission accomplished', he stopped pushing her to eat.

Sue sometimes talked about the time when she first developed the disorder. Sue's parents were killed in he early years of her life and she was raised by her uncle. Some years before we met, her uncle had developed terminal cancer. In order to 'freeze time' and stop her uncle from dying, Sue had turned inward and, in my understanding, the EDM had become activated.

At the beginning, developing a powerful drive towards exercising had felt like a good thing, since it stopped her dwelling on the painful hospice visits to her beloved uncle. And once he died, her new routine of exercise and denial stopped her having to deal with the pain of grief and loss.

Sue reported other ways in which the EDM had made itself important to her. She had always felt intellectually inferior to her peers. The EDM had told her that *it* was the only thing she needed to be confident. She could walk into a room and feel the equal of everyone there. But of course, this was accomplished by the invisible 'glass wall' the disorder had created. A glass wall that kept Sue imprisoned behind it.

Sue began making progress with her relationship with food, and the added energy was helping her with her demanding work commitments. I realised that she was a woman with a great deal of determination. And that this determination was invaluable in changing her relationship with the disorder – the closing hand and the opening hand. Because all this passion was in her healthy self, not the disorder, and she was taking the disorder's energy to fuel her passion for her work.

Here Sue was finally utilising her energy for a constructive purpose. She was spending long hours on revisions before her exams. However she believed she still needed to restrict her fuel intake because she was aware of the action of the disorder. She was afraid that it might suddenly kick in, so she was proceeding cautiously. Here it was not appropriate for me to push her further than she herself knew was safe. A little at a time is better than failure from trying to do too much.

This is why I believe my gentle method, which consciously keeps the disorder 'on board' through negotiation, may be more helpful for the individual than something that attempts to grind the disorder into submission. My own recovery was permanent and final because once I regained control there was no way I wanted to hand control back to the disorder. And it had become reintegrated with the rest of me so it no longer had such power.

Sue was still living with a foot in both camps. She had moments during the day when, she said, she 'woke up', realised her situation and knew that she wanted to disengage the mechanism, but there were still long periods of the day which she saw as 'lost' where she would be so far inside the disorder she didn't remember there was anything beyond it.

At one session she noted that the previous day she had wanted to work and instead was constantly aware of the disorder, nagging, wanting her to nibble and exercise. As always I repeated the simple mantra – separate, negotiate, work to gently take back the energy and control from the disorder – shift the 'normal' to gain weight safely. I reminded her that when she is active, it makes the disorder passive. So have a plan – work on revision for two hours, rest, eat, exercise for half an hour – then return to work.

Obviously since we were seeing each other only two times a week the time in between could seem a long time. This is of course a danger. Any sense of a gap, a void, a break in the person's routine – the disorder rushes in to fill up. If we remember that the disorder is a defence of the body, that it is inside us to *help*, then it makes sense that the mechanism is programmed to fill up any spare space. Which is why it's so helpful to have a plan, and to plan for situations where a void might suddenly open.

It should also be remembered that the EDM, because of its position of standing guard, has a 'first dibs' position on the person's energy. This is why it needs to be addressed actively because otherwise the EDM is the *psyche's default*.

This became apparent when Sue was singled out by her employees to head up a new presentation. She reported that the pitch had gone well – but that afterwards she had been entirely lost in the disorder. In fact, I had warned her of this when she told me of what demands the situation would make on her.

It was clear to me that before the presentation her energy would be focused on it, but that afterwards, in the drop after the rush, the disorder would be there to fill in the gap if she didn't prepare for it. But she had not been able to take this advice. However in the therapy room we were able to consider what information the incident contained: *why* she needed to be more aware of the action of the disorder mechanism.

Once someone has moved past the very early stages of recovery, once they have realised that they have a choice in whether or not the disorder runs their life, they can feel overwhelmed by the situation and their responsibility in it. Again this is an opportunity to reassure and remind the person that at least it is not Armageddon they are involved in – the battle is internal and they *do* have a certain control. The control, as I have said in other places, is gained by becoming *active* which makes the disorder *passive* for a time.

When someone is recovering we have to accept that they will have periods within the day when the disorder is stronger and they feel lost in it. They will only realise how lost they became when they again 'wake up'. The client-centred concept of 'unconditional positive regard' indicates the attitude we need to have towards our clients so that they can re-find for themselves the sense of peace and trust in themselves that we all start off with in life. And 'failures' are just part of the process of eventual success.

Sue talked about how she was planning to eat something for lunch. We agreed that wholewheat bread was more interesting than white. Sue then said that she was frightened. Right now she knew that eating more was what she wanted, but she knew herself of old, that at some point she would find herself back in the action of the disorder. I said that I could well understand her fear – but to take heart in remembering that at some point she *would* wake up, just as she had woken up before.

Once something is really known it can be forgotten again, but there is much more chance that it will also be remembered again. Since Sue had changed in the time she had been coming for sessions she had *changed* – she was not completely the same person. When she had had to go away on business she had not been strong enough not to revert to the demands of the disorder, but even then she had got back on track in a shorter time than the initial sessions – something inside her had retained the understanding.

I am coming to believe that recovery using my approach, in its essence, is permanent. Rather than the temporary fixes where people re-fed will take on enough weight to get away from hospital or other authorities, and then return to starvation and exercise, my method involves an awakening and awareness of self and the action of the disorder. Once this is understood it's almost impossible to truly forget it. Even in the dark ages, a line of knowledge was retained, and in the dark age of the individual, something remains and waits for the right circumstances to come back into the light. Call it the will to live.

A month later Sue again had to go away on business. I said: 'Forewarned is forearmed – you must expect the disorder, with the factor of different circumstances, to be stronger'. This time she was much better prepared. This time she did not listen to the disorder telling her not to eat while travelling. She said it was by no means true that all the time she was in control, but that she was able to be more assertive than previously. She said the previous day she had been able to eat and rest.

We also agreed that she would call me mid-visit. I conjured up an image of telegraph poles. They have to be spaced together enough so that the wire in between doesn't get too slack. Our phone call was the telegraph pole that kept her resolve and understanding from becoming too slack. On the phone she reported that she was enjoying being with her work colleagues. Really talking to them rather than just saying anything until she could get on her own again and exercise. I said this was another positive impression, and that it would lodge in a good place inside her, and take energy from the disorder.

She said yes – and that this was in complete opposition to the disorder who was telling her that *'having no energy was the right way to live'*. Seeing this was very important. She could see that it was not her thinking this crazy thought, but that it made sense that something disordered would have this sort of disordered thinking.

When Sue returned I was amazed to see that even in the brief time she had been away, she had grown more vital in appearance. She had also acquired a tan – this had been the by-product of business meetings held round the hotel pool. This was also significant since previously she had avoided exposing her thin body to public scrutiny.

The only concern Sue expressed at this time was that, having got into a beneficial routine of eating, exercising and resting in between work demands, this would no longer hold now that she was back working towards her academic qualification. I reminded her that previously it was going away on business that had derailed her fragile recovery. So she needed to re-frame the pleasant work-away experience to see that the fact that she had been able to enjoy being round her work colleagues, away from her London routine, showed that her growing understanding and recovery was not just a lucky break: it was real *progress*.

However I also noted to her that she was still taking out more than she was putting back. In one previous session I had offered the image of the feather pillow. Dieting, exercise, handfuls of cereal in place of a proper breakfast – all these things were like handfuls of feathers being pulled out of the pillow. Eventually the pillow would become flat – there wouldn't be any more feathers. This was the position she was at when she began sessions. A central part of recovery was deliberately re-stuffing the pillow with feathers. Which meant eating a little more, resting more, taking back the energy from the disorder.

Sue talked about how she didn't want to lose 'this feeling of life, and how exciting everything is – being able to enjoy being with my work colleagues and not having this voice telling me I needed to be on my own'. She mentioned her pleasure in having the interest and energy to read a book about wild birds – how she had then fallen asleep and that that had also been pleasurable. All these positive impressions being unable to be absorbed by the disorder naturally are absorbed into the healthy self, which action at the same time takes energy away from the disorder.

I said that, like the fact that the book was still there in the morning, her growing sense of awakening would also be there. I reminded her of the usefulness of keeping notes – seeing that you had had the same thought some time previously was helpful in reinforcing the idea that your consciousness was not random, that it had *continuity*.

As always I also reminded Sue of the wisdom of having a plan. The disorder would naturally take up any slack, any void or free space otherwise. She said that when she was away, when she needed to eat with others, the disorder said: 'See – you can't be trusted not to eat' – as though it was a negative. This was another valuable insight into the mechanism of the disorder since it highlighted the *illogicality* of its functioning.

An EDM has no greater plan, no greater purpose. Being mechanical, being part of the moving centre and having the characteristics of unconscious movement, in this example it saw any eating as intrinsically bad. This then related to what Sue had said when she first arrived, that she had a terrible driving force inside which had reduced her life to an overwhelming drive towards starvation and exercise. Now it was as though she was dissecting the mechanism, opening it out and viewing it from a distance, no longer part of it but aware of her growing experience of separation from it.

I repeated the other simple mantra – a certain amount of exercise, taken with the agreement that the disorder would allow her to eat something/re-fuel. Rest and separation from the disorder. And striving to make the decisions of her day herself, staying in her body and not letting the disorder take over.

At another session Sue reported that although she had been able to eat some toast at lunchtime, there was something inside her that was saying strongly that this wasn't necessary. I reminded her that the disorder was in all her centres – thinking, emotional, moving and instinctive – and that of course it reacted automatically to the thought of food. I said that she needed to accept that, because the disorder had become deeply entrenched over the previous twelve years, she would still feel its presence strongly.

It is also important to remember that the disorder was *frightened*. Any thought of food, and the physical energy change or just the presence of food in the body was like the image of the matter spilled onto the clean white paper. It was like a dirty floor that needed immediate cleaning. The disorder is severely limited in its scope and as well as being a bully it is a coward.

Therefore a way of understanding it, and more importantly, a way of controlling it, is to feel sorry for it. Poor disorder, only trying to do what it's been created for. Once you have pity for something you change your attitude to it. Just as being active makes the disorder passive, feeling sorry for its misunderstood sense of responsibility obviously places it in a subservient position where it can be controlled rather than the controlling force.

The following session Sue, with downcast expression, related the details of an unexpected event. Her work mates had surprised her with a birthday celebration. Although she had been thrilled, she was suddenly struck by an internal fear that she was not prepared, was not capable of accepting all the attention. She had been unable to stop herself becoming aggressive in perfectly ordinary conversation. Eventually she had had to blame it on a headache and made a discreet exit.

We talked about the incident *purely as information*. This is an important point because otherwise we may divide events into success or failure. In fact all are information and we can be dispassionate about finding the truth and insight in each. The incident was a clear example of why it was unhealthy and unhelpful for Sue to live her life in the disorder. The disorder is very narrow in focus, and obviously the person doesn't have as much energy as we all require for daily tasks. Because the disorder had been unable to *budget* for the surprise, it was thrown on its few resources. And so

Sue had flipped into negativity. Rather than keeping Sue safe, as promised, the EDM had exposed why it cannot be trusted.

I said the best way to regard the upset she had felt – 'it was horrible'- was just to note the mechanics of the disorder and try to resolve how she could remember this in future. I asked what she had eaten today? 'My normal amount - a grapefruit and a cup of cereal with water.'

I replied gently that that was enough for someone on a strict diet. It was interesting to see that the disorder had persuaded her to believe that that sort of intake was adequate for someone requiring a 'normal' amount of energy. But instead she needed to understand she was still very much eating as a compromise and that she needed to be clear with the disorder that the food was a compromise. In this way *she* was negotiating for more, rather than accepting the disorder's idea of what was normal food intake.

I wondered if the upsetting incident regarding the surprise party would be another breakthrough. For someone whose sense of self is constantly strained through the presence of a disorder, arriving at a resolution and being able to stick to it is very difficult. But at least when they do, it is *their* understanding. A strong impression like this would most probably leave a 'taste' which she would want to avoid in future.

At the next session I talked about my growing understanding that the disorder was an actual mechanism – like hay fever - with similar drawbacks. I also talked about the concept of containment and nameless dread. That the baby, unable to make sense of its fears, projects onto its mother all these *indigestible* fears and that if the mother isn't able to contain them, these come back as 'nameless dread' (Bion). So that someone growing up with a sense of nameless dread was subconsciously opening doors to rooms in their psyche – one of which might contain the EDM.

This had a big effect on Sue. She related that she had gone to see a film with an attractive man. Although the evening was going well she had noticed herself becoming snappy, negative and internally blaming. So rather than going with the negativity, she had had something to eat at the cinema. Even that small amount of food caused her consciousness to change, and she could see how far the disorder had already taken over.

The film began. For a while she found it difficult to watch because she had felt horribly confused. After an hour, the feeling suddenly cleared and she had been able to enjoy the film and the company of her new friend.

I said that these two thoughts – 'nameless dread' and seeing how food could help her – were linked. The key, as she had discovered, was fuel and a little space to allow the instinctive and emotional centres to sort things out.

An aspect of people with disorders is that they are invariably much harder on themselves than other people. Sometimes this leads to self-harm or bulimia (see next chapter); sometimes they are just not aware of how harshly they think and treat themselves. But here Sue had seen that by taking a space, resting and giving herself a little nourishment she was able to regain herself. She had finally given in to her fragile self, rather than being harsh. And she would continue to gain from being kinder to herself. Loving herself and liking herself was a highly beneficial element of her recovery.

The next session Sue noted that she was only a few days away from her exam. I cautioned her – again forewarned is forearmed – that once the adrenalin rush of the event had passed she would be vulnerable to the action of the disorder, rushing in to fill the emotional and work void. She said she was aware of this, but she was scared the disorder would 'jump' her.

I reminded her of the closed and opening hands. Now that the disorder was weaker, now the healthy self was stronger, she had more on her side – like taking the other side's chess pieces.

The following session was several days after the exam. Sue reported that she had been much more strongly aware of the disorder. I said this was only to be expected - the clear thoughts she had been experiencing were partly due to all the energy her creative drive was taking from the disorder. Without it, she would need to more closely monitor the disorder. I suggested she keep a journal – 'a diary of memories and healing' – which if she got as passionate about keeping it as she had been about preparing for her exam would be a great help in taking energy from the disorder. She said she would think about it. Basically she was scared that the disorder would now come right back in and she would again be lost.

Sue arrived at the next session quite bright. She said her 'film friend' was going away and she had spent a couple of days with him. She had also gone out with a group of his friends. This experience then proved useful in what was to follow.

Picking up on something she had said, I asked her if she didn't really *want* to disengage the EDM. She said it was more that the EDM was saying – for example in social situations – that the *EDM was giving her confidence*. I thought this a very interesting statement. I didn't argue with it, and instead asked Sue how this 'sense of confidence' felt to her.

Tears filled her eyes. She said she found it hard to think of how she had appeared in social situations over the last twelve years. That when she had floated into a room with anorexia, she felt like an *angel*. She took nothing in, she participated passively, and all the time she wanted only to go back to her own, lonely, room.

She told me that for many years she had had the image of being an angel. 'If only I can be an angel. Angels don't need food'. Again here was the mindset of the disorder – only this time Sue had enough presence to be aware that she didn't *want* to be a angel. She had enjoyed being with her friend's circle – she found the idea of being *awake*, of having a physical presence in a social situation exciting and unknown.

I said – true. Meeting people, especially strangers, is both exhilarating and there is a sense of mystery – even perhaps the danger of a *faux pas*. But that it was a normal part of life and that was one reason people in social situations drank alcohol and smoked. *Many people need to feel a confidence they don't really have in public situations.* Sue said that yes, she was scared of the downside – but that overall she felt positive about the prospects of being herself in public.

Before Sue's next session I reflected that she had really only been working on recovery since the end of June. This was now the beginning of November, so only four short months. I remembered her having asked me how long it had taken me, and my saying six months. At this point I wondered how she would be in two months.

The next session gave me my answer. Sue related that she had spent the weekend with her man friend. She had experienced herself as being 'wide awake' – that this meant that she 'just couldn't be bothered to do the work of the disorder'. She also said that this, and other emotional and intellectual experiences she'd been having, 'were strange, a bit frightening'.

I recalled to her that when I had been growing up, near the beach and sea in Durban, a girl called Paula had been somewhat mocked by the group because every now and again she wanted to sit on rocks and look out to sea, on her own. It was termed 'fashionably alone'. But in fact what she was doing was heeding a call from inside, to get in touch with a deeper part of herself.

This was similar to what Sue was going through now. As the energy came back from the disorder, various parts or voices in her were waking up and having their moment. I suggested she think of them as subjective intellectual and emotional moments or states. Some would pass, some would have more staying power. I compared these with the reason why some people take drugs – to experience different inner states: 'You're having these without having to take drugs!'

I also compared it to the sensation, if we've been resting on an arm, of blood coming back into the hand. 'Pins and needles' *hurts*. The subjective intellectual and emotional states, on the other hand, didn't actually hurt: they were just different. It was the difference that caused a sense of fear.

And here Sue needed to remember two things. Firstly 'nameless dread'. If there was no real cause for fear, for her to just think of it as nameless dread, and not feel burdened to respond to it. Secondly that the fear was only the sense of the unfamiliar. The disorder would always label this a cause for alarm – 'so give me your energy and I will keep you safe'.

But as Sue went on to say, what was really apparent to her was the ridiculousness of the disorder's Promise: 'When I think of the number of times I haven't done just ordinary stuff – like going out for a meal or something spontaneous – just because I had this thing inside saying *don't* eat, and *you have to go home and exercise* …!'

Clearly Sue has moved far away from the direct influence of the disorder. Although she is wise to be wary, her understanding grows and nurtures her new direction in life – to have a life. Remembering that it had been only four months since she had had to start again, and the pressures she had been through not only from her job but her additional study, for her to have moved this far was highly gratifying to both of us.

Sue went on to talk about her immediate plans. She wanted to enjoy the prospect of a relationship with her film friend, whose name is Bill. And she was looking for new work opportunities. 'I just want to rest, refuel, enjoy my life'. I said that sounded great. It was the disorder that had told her that she was so terribly special she couldn't live a normal life like other people. As she was returning more and more to a proper perspective, she could see that she didn't want to be 'special' anymore.

And the mechanism, which woke up to save Sue the pain of losing her beloved relative and instead became the instrument of a waking nightmare, can be seen to be disengaging.

CHAPTER SEVEN

Case Study: Bulimia
'The Quality of the Relationship'

Adam is above average height, with black hair and piercing brown eyes. Unlike Sue whose physical appearance left no doubt as to her issue, Adam when he first came to sessions looked healthy and well turned out. Once he began to talk about himself a picture emerged of his internal state that differed from the charming and polite exterior. A person riddled with anger, guilt and grief, trapped in a daily routine of bingeing and purging.

Adam's parents are divorced and his mother had vowed never to marry again. Instead, she had decided, she would seek emotional fulfilment by raising her child and working with children. Adam reports that his mother is a warm and sensitive woman who has only his best interests at heart. When she was younger Adam's mother had had emotional issues and Adam knows she is stricken with guilt that she might inadvertently have caused her son's problems.

In the period before he began attending for sessions Adam had left the family home and had lived 'semi-independently', working for a family friend. However this arrangement broke down and Adam was now back with his mother.

Adam has a loving girlfriend, Beth, who is always very willing to listen to him talking about his illness. Adam sometimes feels that she is his carer rather than his girlfriend – sometimes he likes this and sometimes not.

We had a breakthrough in the fourth session – where Adam let go and revealed to me how very ill he actually was. He had become so used to hiding the truth of the severity of his disorder from those around him that it had taken him some testing time with me before he felt able to let go of even a little of what was happening inside.

I had a moment of internal panic. As he described the wretchedness and violence of his daily life, the heaviness of feeling and the enormous rage and resentment inside him broke across me like a wave and I temporarily floundered. I thought: 'This is too heavy for me – he should be in an institution'. A moment later I recovered and thought: 'But that would be exactly what I am against – someone else would be making his decisions for him'. Instead I was able to stay with my experience and beliefs – that he should negotiate with the illness.

Separation, negotiation, one flower closing and the other opening. I repeated the mantra several times and Adam responded positively to it. My moment of doubt passed and with it came more strength in the simplicity and truth of the idea. My own experience showed me that taking someone's control away might not be the best way to help them. But being able to *listen* as they spoke out their internal torment provided a safe haven. Up till now Adam's 'haven' had been the relief vomiting gave him. Now the quality of our relationship might be able to take its place.

Adam would never come across as ugly, or vain, or a bad person – any of the things he so readily labelled himself. What he saw as gross indulgence was often, from my perspective, no more than someone struggling to find himself against a background of other voices – a number of professionals who had challenged and inadvertently confused his sense of self. I knew that only Adam was able to really understand what was going on inside him, and that therefore I would be most helpful just by repeating my simple formula, and allowing him to rest on the island created by the warm and supportive relationship that began to grow between and around us.

One thing he found difficult to reveal was his history of 'polygamy' around women. When he had been at catering school – a short-lived passion - he had enjoyed relationships with two women; one who lived in a flat opposite him, and one whose work based her in Paris, so she was able to see him only sporadically. Adam related that 'enjoyed' was not the word: it was at this point that his bulimia was at its very worst. He was eating, purging and starving.

Since I had been anorexic but not bulimic I was very interested to understand the difference. I remember, and I shared with Adam, the one time when I'd had the idea to throw up. But I couldn't, I lacked the know-how to force it and didn't have much energy behind the thought. Adam was different. He spoke about himself in such abusive terms, it was clear that throwing up and cleaning up his own vomit struck him as just about right for such a 'bad' person. He recounted how it had felt, 'cheating' on his Paris-based girlfriend and being light-headed from starvation and the violence of purging.

A few sessions in, Adam told me he and his girlfriend had decided to 'take a break'. Beth wanted him to be well and thought that being on his own would help this. The idea was that this would allow him to be true to himself rather than having to worry about another person. This idea also needed to be extended to his friends. As one would expect with such an attractive and lively person, Adam had a big social circle. But he confessed during a session that he was finding the strain of having to be 'ill for them' a burden.

We explored this. It appeared that Adam's friends, well-meaning and sympathetic, were inadvertently pressurising him to keep coming up with stories of how out of control his life was. I suggested that he not say anything about what was going on to anyone except his mother and perhaps Beth. I said that the way I saw it, his internal life was his own, he wasn't 'on view' and it wasn't his job to make his friends feel good for being sympathetic.

This was the first time that Adam got to think of himself as being able to hold something inside. Clearly this idea generally has great importance for bulimics, who struggle to keep food inside. Until I said that it *wasn't necessary* Adam had felt obliged to open up every aspect of his illness with his friends. But now he decided to hold back, allowing a private and *trusting part* of himself to grow. Since part of the reason Adam displayed such self-hatred was that

'I know I can't trust myself, I can't be responsible', being responsible to himself about not sharing his inner life with all and sundry was a start.

At this point two women came into Adam's life. One was the old girlfriend from catering school, the other a dynamic woman he had met at a party. His feelings towards his old girlfriend were contradictory and reflected Adam's preferred way of operating which was to avoid confrontation, even confronting his own emotions. Gently we began to address what he really felt about his old girlfriend and Adam acknowledged the impossibility of their maintaining a friendship with safe boundaries.

The woman he had met at the party, Sally, became more of a focus point. Adam saw himself as despicable and untrustworthy in that Beth did not know about this event – but I saw that Adam was wracked with guilt and as we explored in the session, neither Beth nor anyone else *owned* Adam: if he wanted to pursue an interest in Sally, as a free agent and adult he was entitled to. This incident also helped me to understand the bulimic way of processing situations: his disorder was adamant that having feelings for Sally was proof positive of Adam's base and despicable nature. The purging had increased and now Adam no longer needed to force himself. Just crouching over a toilet brought up whatever food he had inside.

Even this aspect of bulimia is seized upon by the disorder as evidence of how bad the person is. Adam said: 'What kind of person needs to crouch in front of a toilet and bring up bile before they can have any food?' To me, only an ill one. To the disorder, only a bad one who deserved every bit of their discomfort and anguish.

It is probably clear to you, by now, that in the way in which the bulimic disorder is structured and manifests it is different from the anorexic. Although there is evidence that one sort and the other becomes blurred – bulimic anorexics or anorexic bulimics – there is an additional pain, an additional self-inflicted torture in bulimia. Perhaps it is only luck that caused me to be anorexic only, because bulimia presents as an even worse manifestation. I remember wanting to reward myself for taking off weight, but I didn't beat up on myself for 'ugly' thoughts.

'Ugly' thoughts to a bulimic are often in the realm of what, I said to Adam, seems like a *skewed sense of responsibility*. Whereas having a strong moral code is seen as praiseworthy, to a bulimic the moral code is merciless. Adam's disorder punished him severely for being so wilful as to attempt to explore his sexual and emotional needs. We must always bear in mind the narrowness of the disorder's remit and how everything outside this is perceived as a threat or to be wrong.

Therefore it was also very important that in our sessions we gave due attention to Adam's hesitant reports of how he was feeling his way forward emotionally. Wracked with guilt over his mixed-up feeling for Beth, desperate for the sense of lightness and pleasure he experienced in his brief moments of friendship with Sally, Adam's skewed sense of responsibility and punitive moral code turned what for most others would have been a natural exploration into a battlefield of constant pain. He reported severe stomach cramps, migraines and manifestations of a compromised immune system.

Although the emotional entanglement, and the bulimia's harsh punishments, made exactly what was happening inside Adam harder to keep focused on, it didn't change the way I addressed his situation. I suggested that he write down simple words or phrases, perhaps a word that meant something only to him, since his mother habitually cleaned his room to keep some semblance of order.

The first sign of a gradual shift in Adam's relationship to his disorder came when he took a job for one day a week in a local bakery. Since Adam was used to spending long periods of time cooped up in his room , he greeted the idea of having a reason to get out the house with hope – and apprehension. Previously he had not been able to hold down a job. But now, he hoped that our sessions would make the necessary difference.

How the sessions were helping became clear when he casually announced one day that he was 'thinking of self-harming'. He had had periods of this in his teens and it had given him relief. I was thoughtful, then I told him about something someone else had once told me. That this person had gone to visit a friend, and the friend was wearing a t-shirt. Visible on the friend's arms was an angry wound, still open and weeping. Yet the friend said nothing about the wound and the person who related the story to me was dumbstruck.

I offered this story only as information. I did not make a judgement or even try to interpret either that story, or what might have brought Adam to make the comment about self-harming thoughts. The incident was as un-dramatic as if we had been discussing when to next meet. What I did say was that it didn't surprise me to hear him say something like this. Since there was something – some change – happening inside him, it was only to be expected that inside a new voice – in this case self-harming – would speak up, assessing whether it was their turn to manifest.

Adam did not self-harm and the subject never came up again. But if Adam was in a way testing me, to find out if I really could hear what was going on inside him and *not* over-react the way others had, then he had his answer.

Adam was conscious of wanting to do right by Beth. He was struggling. This was not a case of guilt, this was a real attempt, made harder by the ongoing demands of his disorder, to do right for both of them. He just felt more right about Sally. Yet even though Sally had indicated a strong desire for Adam to think of her as his girlfriend, Adam wanted to be alone, to concentrate on his recovery. He was finding the job – which had quickly trebled to three days a week – difficult since he spent every day with pain from his stomach. He was eating a small amount, but not negotiating with the disorder. Rather he was waiting until there was no more time, then forcing food down and going back to work.

I stressed the importance of keeping the disorder 'on side'. Understanding that the disorder was part of the body's defence system, appreciating that it was trying to do a job, would have made it possible for him to think of the disorder with compassion. This would aid his recovery in that he would not be adding to the battle by being in constant fear that the disorder would manifest inappropriately – for example if fellow workers cottoned on to the real reason he needed to use the bathroom.

Although Adam said that spending a little time with Sally made him feel stronger and able to face the disorder, the disorder was punishing him. He started to lose weight. At this point he went away for a couple of weeks and when he returned I could see he had lost about a stone. He told me that the previous day he had spent several hours eating and throwing up: 'It just seemed inevitable'.

I explained that when he took in food, that began a cycle. Since the EDM is rooted in the moving centre, it seeks to manifest through *movement*. By not addressing the disorder, by not negotiating with it to retain the fuel so he could do his job, he was starting a cycle. Eventually, even if he no longer wanted to be sick, he felt it inevitable and it happened. Because the disorder was in all his centres and had a lot of power, so even when he no longer desired to vomit, the disorder had set the cycle in motion, and it was only a matter of time.

Of course, having been physically sick he then was hungry again. And again by not negotiating with the disorder, the new food would again start the cycle, so that he was still not retaining the nourishment of the food.

I said that he needed to remember that he was not in control, the disorder was. And that even when he believed he was having a 'good day' – rust never sleeps and neither does a disorder.

I talked about the concept of 'containment'. As I've said elsewhere in this book, the idea is that the baby, unable to process its own fears etc, projects them onto the containing object – the mother. If the mother is unable to contain, it comes back to the baby as 'nameless dread'. Adam had often talked about exactly this, saying he didn't know *why* he felt bad, only that he did. And it appeared that this may have been a large cause of the disorder 'waking up': the constant pressure of nameless dread had led the psychic system to believe that the disorder was needed in order to give Adam relief from his constant anxiety.

Adam found this concept very interesting and could see how it fitted in. Adam's relationship with his mother, though loving and constructive for the most part, was also another source of despair and pain. Fundamentally he believed he could not forgive his mother for her attempts to help over the years. He would say: 'If only she had understood that I didn't want an outside expert – I wanted *her* to tell me to pull myself together'. He knew her to be a warm and caring person but there were times he would say that he believed she *didn't* want him to get better, so that she would always have to look after him.

At these times it was important both to absolutely hear and acknowledge Adam's depth of feeling, and then to offer hope in the form of counter-proof. When Adam, in a frenzy of grief, stated that he really and truly believed he was staying ill because that's what his mother wanted, it helped to recall that he had previously talked about how he had been moved by her genuine pleasure when he was having a good day, or how it had saddened her to see he was bingeing and purging. At no time did I ever hear real evidence of this 'bad' mother – like Klein's 'bad breast – but to deny Adam's reality on this would have confused his growing sense of emotional identity.

At this point Adam was still trying to make up his mind between Beth and Sally, and working (now down to) two days a week in the bakery. But to listen to Adam talking it was as though he was running the United Nations. His skewed sense of responsibility, his sense of the dramatic that blew up the smallest event, indicated that the disorder was keeping Adam in confusion by making any small thing of great importance. Clearly this was a disorder manifestation different to the anorexic, who often wants to get through life with as little fuss as possible.

Since the disorder was giving him 'the small life lived big', I wanted to use this to help overcome its manifestation. I reminded him that rather than try and eat 'normally' Adam should eat a little, and negotiate with the disorder that this was 'fuel' necessary for work. In this way he might not set off the cycle that ended in purging and relief. Here I noted that, of course, the 'relief' was mainly that felt by the disorder, since in reality he was still underweight and really did need the food for nourishment.

What did it mean, to have Adam begin as a normal-weight bulimic, then move to a thinner physical appearance? Since I don't include the weighing of clients, which would in any case be highly inappropriate for a therapist working as I do, I didn't know exactly how much weight Adam had lost. He was still the better person to decide on this issue. He told me that he had wanted to put on weight, in response to negative comments from friends – and had put on half a stone 'of crap'.

The idea that 'weight' is the ideal by which recovery can be measured is not a simple statement. In this instance, by eating sweets and other non-nurturing substances Adam had put on 'desirable weight' – but it had left him feeling bloated and unhealthy. Here also it was interesting to see the *kind* of food the disorder prefers – high-calorie, non-nurturing or sustaining, junk food (nowadays politely termed 'snack food'). Isn't it interesting to understand that, logically, a disorder would want only disordered food?

Therefore the way for Adam to put on a little weight was not to follow the dictates and fancies of the disorder, but to concentrate on eating a little something of a more nurturing foodstuff – with negotiation.

Emotionally, the reason why Adam had taken weight off suddenly at this point was, once again, his skewed sense of responsibility. He revealed in the next session that he believed that, when he told Beth it was over between them, if he was thin she *would not be able to be angry with him*. I said that I was aware that weight-wise we were 'moving closer to the edge'. He said that in fact he felt he had been gradually losing weight since we had first started working together and that it was a sign that he now felt confident enough to show other people that he really was sick.

Bulimia is an eating disorder that often disguises its severity. Because 'normal weight bulimics' appear to be able to eat 'properly', the fact that they vomit up much of what they consume keeps them more or less stable. But they are in reality absorbing less than proper nourishment and are suffering the effects of a continual lack of food similarly to an anorexic. Adam had said that by losing weight he was showing that he was feeling more confident, more able to have his inner and outer selves fit. Yet he was also doing it to display his vulnerability to Beth. But finally it was not for me to demand that he put weight on, or to see this development as a regression. I had to go with his perception, and respect his growing feeling of confidence, despite the seeming contradiction in his physical appearance.

However, I said that I was still concerned that he was not fully *engaging* with the disorder. He had found ways of compromising with it but that is not the same thing. The problem with finding a way to work with the disorder but *not* disengaging it is akin to having an elephant in a small room. Yes you can squirm round it and occasionally you and it will be on good terms but eventually if you want a normal life it has to go.

Previously Adam had said that what really worked for him was for someone on the outside to say something powerful. At this time there had been in the press coverage of a tragic Brazilian model who had died from starvation and the effects of anorexia. I said to Adam that I had read various reports to the effect that between six and twenty five per cent of people with long term eating disorders *die* of the illness. Obviously this was not something I would say to a client at the first session when their confusion is at its worst. But sobering fact can help put a complicated situation into perspective.

Adam said that yes, saying that had helped. I had noticed before how he never argued with what I offered. That was because it was *offered*. It was never an ultimatum or a confrontation. He knew that he was not coming to sessions to look good or look bad for me. He understood that we were two people with a single agenda: his recovery. This meant that rather than take my bringing up of this statistic as my pessimistic view of his situation, it was said so that there were no secrets between us. It was a fact, and it was just a fact. It was there for him if he found it useful, but it was not there to force him to do anything he was doing differently – only his own desire to do things differently would accomplish that.

About this time Adam broke off finally with his girlfriend Beth. She had behaved magnificently in a difficult situation and

Adam hoped they would remain on friendly terms. Understand-
ably, Beth needed time to be on her own and Adam could see the
sense in this.

He carefully explained to me that he did not want to quickly
move on to Sally. Sally was being understanding and undemanding
and this Adam appreciated. Having previously felt bad about the
way relationships had ended it was particularly important to him
that this one should end as well as possible, and that he should feel
honourable rather than bad. Therefore he did not rush into a full
relationship with Sally, and went through a period of mourning for
his lost relationship with Beth.

From the point of view of his recovery, this was excellent. Here
was a situation that Adam himself was in charge of, and given the
opportunity he was doing it in a responsible way. This gave him the
invaluable experience of *feeling good about himself* – while denying
the disorder the energy it would have taken should Adam's 'skewed
sense of responsibility' and punishment have had the chance to
manifest.

Yet it needs to be emphasised that here, as continually
expressed in our meetings, Adam felt weighed down by a dispro-
portionate sense of 'nameless dread'. He could appreciate that his
handling of the present situation marked a big change in his previous dealings. From the beginning of our working together he had
said that he would do anything to avoid confrontation, that he
always ran away. Now he was standing and taking responsibility but
he was still full of negativity, anger and conflicting feelings. Some
of these were still concerning his mother.

From one session to the next Adam would move between a
compassionate understanding that his mother had done her best,
and that she did genuinely love him. and his sense of anger that
she had not got it right for him. He would be charmed with a gra-
cious gesture she had made, but then dashed by something she
had done – mostly not even concerning Adam. It became clear
that Adam could not really give up the action of the disorder as
long as he could not bear to give up his conflicted feelings towards
his mother.

This may seem that I believe that the person themselves *is* in control of the EDM, that it is a dual conspiracy against the world. No. I believe that the action of the EDM specifically is beyond the control of the person affected unless they negotiate with it. However what is true is that the person, particularly in a situation where the disorder has been active for a long time, has grown so used to the presence of the disorder, and has their emotional and intellectual functions so enmeshed with it, that the person finds they do not know what is them and what is disorder. So they do believe that it is they who are operating the EDM. It is only when the person can separate from it that they realise *the EDM* is actually in charge. The separation is the first stage, after which the process of disengaging the EDM begins.

Adam talked about the title of a book he had seen on a library shelf, 'A Gradual Awakening', at the next session. He said that this is how he thought of the recovery process. He said my idea of 'a little, and real' could be expressed as a gradual awakening. I agreed.

At this session Adam also mentioned that his mother was due for an award for services to children's education. He said he was pleased about this. But it seemed that there was another thought, and this took some time to emerge. It was only when Adam felt completely reassured that I would not judge him that he was able to say that he had felt extremely angry when he heard about the award: 'She's getting an award for helping other children – and she's never been able to help me!' Here was the ongoing, angry psychic wound revealed between us.

I knew that it didn't help to argue rationally. To remind him of the many times his mother had got it spectacularly right. The wound needed air in our sessions, to breathe, for the light to shine on it and hopefully effect a change in how he felt. Adam was sensitive, charming, attractive to many people – and suffering. However much I might want to 'turn off' his suffering it wouldn't work – that's what the years in other therapies had shown him. Therefore his feelings in this situation should just remain where they were. This allowed that part of him to feel expressed, after which the voice no longer needed to make itself heard.

What I did say was, since he had deliberately taken off weight so that Beth couldn't be angry when he broke up with her, would he now consider this 'mission accomplished' and try to put on weight? He said he was trying to, that family members had mentioned the weight loss and that he didn't feel physically happy being underweight.

The easy way in which we could talk about his weight situation meant that he could hear my opinion and not over-react. It was part of the flow of conversation between us. How different this would have been if the session began with him being weighed. Clearly there would have been conflict, with the disorder on his side driving a wedge between us. This way 'weight' was a normal part of our conversation, and did not have undue and possibly unhelpful emphasis.

Additionally, an aspect of our relationship is the *humour* that often characterised our sessions. Humour, used appropriately, can cut through deep and painful feeling.

When Adam first introduced the idea of Sally, I hadn't been able to suppress as smile. A similar smile appeared on Adam's face. He said that he appreciated my response since he wasn't finding the subject easy to talk about. This didn't mean that either of us wasn't taking it seriously, just that to approach every stage and every element of a client's life with grimness may feel overwhelming.

A little lightness helped because the situation was already complicated in that Beth had returned and was trying her best to affect a reconciliation. Adam described in detail a difficult and complex discussion lasting several hours that had taken place the night before. I was struck by the detail of how Adam had handled the surprise confrontation: 'You know what you did? You *contained* it. You were able to contain both of you, and the situation!'

Adam caught on immediately. Instinctively he had been able to do for himself what he had spent many years trying to force his mother to do: contain. In this session Adam was the most positive I had yet seen him. He could now see that he did not need to rely on the disorder to run his emotional life: he was starting to take control for himself.

The next session, however, Adam had somewhat regressed in terms of his confidence. This sort of waxing and waning is only to be expected: recovery is not a straightforward path. Sally was away on business and he dreaded her return, since he again thought he looked 'rubbish'. He was trying to put on weight, by eating junk food. This in turn made him feel bloated and uncomfortable, with a continual sick feeling. 'But it's the only thing the disorder will allow me to eat'.

There it was again: the disorder, being a disorder, could stomach only high-calorie, low-nourishment food, which had a quick burnout. Nourishing food was regarded as the enemy because it changed the sense of the body from being highly wired to something where energy was burned up in a slower, more useful way.

I said that *anyone* who was eating the sort of junk food he was would feel exactly like he did. It's often helpful to enlarge the particular into the universal. Just as with saying to my anorexic client that exercise *could* have a useful function, so saying that anyone would have the same reaction to so much junk food was helpful because it broke down the idea of Adam being 'special' and allowed him to see he was like everyone else.

This was another facet of Adam's complex psychic make-up. As well as being bad and debasing himself, he also had a strong demand to be 'special'. For a long time he was not able to take the sort of simple jobs available to him because they were 'beneath him' and did not give him the cachet of being special.

This self-aggrandising and self-debasement, going together, can be observed in other manifestations of internal conflict – for example a young woman I know who went for a job interview and told the person leading the panel that what she really wanted was *their* job. She lasted only a few days since there was a too great a gap between her vision and her reality. (This is also observable in, for example, American Idol where certain hapless persons' illusions about their singing ability are heartlessly exposed as 'entertainment'). With Adam, having both these polar beliefs was being reinforced by the disorder, since swinging between these extremes kept

Adam unstable – and that instability suited the disorder and made it feel safe and in control.

Sally returned and everything had been fine. At our next session Adam said that he still couldn't relax. Even though on paper he had what he thought he wanted, he couldn't relax because he was still so angry with his mother. I offered the ideas of Melanie Klein, the theory of containment and how the relationship with the mother was seen as primary in importance. Although it was more usually ascribed to the relationship between *girls* or women and their mother, it was obviously just as true for Adam. Raising the subject immediately brought out Adam's old anger, his sense of wild grief that his mother had not been able to give him what he needed.

We talked about how his relationship with food might be mirroring his relationship with his mother. That his separation/ independence from his mother might be being played out in his need/rejection and ejection of food. It was important that I didn't come to any conclusions. I am not Adam and it is for him to under-stand what is true.

At this point Adam went to spend a few days with his father. He said he looked forward to this because his father would force him to eat properly. I said that this was not taking the EDM into consid-eration, that it would be better rather than force food down if he negotiated with it: 'I need fuel in order to be able to live my day'. He went to his father and kept food down, but was continually uncomfortable and in stomach pain. This shows how you cannot *force* the EDM and expect it to compromise.

At this time I also went away, to New York. The different perspective helped me to further define my developing theories. As a result I came to understand the nature of the EDM in a slightly different way. Previously, and as I had written on my website, I had regarded the EDM as an artificial centre that thrived by taking energy from the four proper centres – the intellectual, emotional, moving and instinctive. Now I realised that, given the characteris-tics, the disorder is a defence mechanism which is a function of the *moving* centre.

110

The characteristics I looked at are the fight/flight mechanism (where instinct, not thought, is the decider) and the fact that the disorder expresses itself in some sort of movement. And that although it does not have a thinking brain, it is clearly able to think in much the same way as an animal would. I talked about this to Adam and he became physically moved: tears gathered in his eyes.

Out of this came another breakthrough. Adam spoke a few, half-finished sentences and I spliced these together and gave them back to him. Adam was staying ill *until his mother learned how to look after him*. That he was spending all his energy keeping himself vulnerable until his mother did or said what was necessary to make him safe.

We talked about what this meant, and how he was using all his energy *to fight the wrong battle*. It was one that could never be won, and it was taking the energy needed for the real 'battle' – recovery. It was clear the battle could never be won because Adam then gave examples of how his mother *did* get things very right, sometimes putting Adam's needs ahead of her own even at moments which put her under a great strain.

I said that it seemed that whatever it was inside Adam keeping him in this frozen state, whatever his mother did would *never* make a difference. The hurt was too young, too deep, too unconscious for anything to affect it. Could he now stop trying to fight this internal battle, this lose-lose situation, and use his energy to save himself?

Previously Adam had mentioned that the GP he had seen at the eating disorders unit of his local hospital had given him a prescription for Prozac. Adam said that he was completely and utterly opposed to the idea of taking Prozac. That he could not bear the idea of something like that entering his body and taking control. This was particularly interesting to hear because an anorexic client had said basically the same thing. It appeared that, either coming from the disorder, or from the person's disordered sense of being, the idea of something artificial entering the system was deemed completely unacceptable even though it had been prescribed by a doctor.

Widening this to encompass therapy as a whole, the reason people who might benefit from the right therapy most often give for not seeking professional help is they don't want to 'become someone else'. As I would say to someone in a more general therapeutic context, it won't change you into someone else, it will help you become *more of yourself*. To Adam I said also that, specifically because patients had formerly become addicted to things like Valium, GPs were very careful to monitor the dosage and the prescription would be for only a limited supply. Adam heard this but he remained unconvinced about the desirability of taking a pill to help him even temporarily.

At his next session Adam reported that the understanding that he was keeping himself ill until his mother worked out how to cure him had stayed with him. We talked about the nature of the EDM. How with anorexia it manifests through diet and exercise, with bulimia through intake and purging. He said that what I hadn't included was the ongoing tension in his throat which is relieved by throwing up. He said that at the homeopathic clinic where he receives support they told him that the reason he experiences tension in his throat was that he was habitually shallow breathing, using only the upper part of his chest.

There is an exercise, useful for singers, to help correct the location of breathing. The candle exercise. Hold your finger a foot away from your mouth, point the index finger up as though it was a candle and blow it out. The diaphragm automatically contracts from the stomach, thus correcting the breathing. Adam tried this and liked the sensation. Since it's so simple I include it here for anyone with a similar problem.

Adam talked about how he thought he might want to work in the shop, 'working with people' - rather than in the bakery itself. Apparently when he raised this with his work colleagues they didn't take him seriously, since he was always cancelling dates with friends and they didn't think he was 'a people person'. But I heard that he was attracted by the idea of giving to people, in this case giving service in the shop.

At the next session Adam revealed that he was starting to help at the bakery shop counter. He also said that he was now taking the Prozac.

The following session Adam reported that he was moving up to four days a week at the bakery, mainly on the customer service side. He began the session by saying how good he was feeling and that this came from the sense of feeling really fulfilled in his work. Working on the bakery side had not given him this. I said that it shouldn't be forgotten that he had learned a great deal about *how* to hold down a job during those months in the kitchen. Now he was ready for a more responsible position – and this also meant he could see that he would be more financially independent. It is important to note here that previously Adam was unable to consider a simple job like working in a shop – now he *was* doing it and just holding it down was again giving him a sense of self-respect.

Taking the Prozac he said was a great help in that it had quietened the tortuous voices that tossed him one way and another, particularly over his relationship with his mother. He reported that he was relieved to discover the Prozac was not making him feel strange or different, just that it gave him relief. Just as I have encouraged clients to also be working with a nutritionalist as well as having therapy, obviously therapy works well in combination with medical support (and in some instances it would be unhealthy or potentially damaging to have only therapy without medical support).

Yet I must confess and said it to him that I didn't want it to feel as though all he had really needed, after the journey we had been through together, was Prozac!

Adam became serious. 'You are the only one I stayed with', he said. 'Because before you, there was no one I could trust. No one who I could talk to about the thoughts and feelings I believed were bad and unacceptable'. When Adam began he said over and over that there was nothing inside him he could trust. Having found strength and belief in himself through my responses to him in just the few months we had worked together, he now felt capable of handling a relationship responsibly, and capable of holding down a job.

I reacted to his words with modesty. I tried to make a joke, remembering that the comedienne Sandra Bernhard had produced a light-hearted book for which her friend Madonna had done a cover blurb. The blurb – sending up a trend in life coaching books – read: 'This book saved my life – Madonna'. Once I said this I thought I might have got it wrong, that Adam might think I was putting words in his mouth.

Instead he said: 'No, that's right. You *have* saved my life. And when you write your book (this book) I'll say so'.

It was then that I had the idea of calling this chapter *the quality of the relationship*. We never really know what is going to help – although I am more and more certain what does not. I remembered the words of Martha Graham, the distinguished American dancer and choreographer: 'Where a dancer stands – that spot is holy ground' (de Mille, 1991, p. 96).

This is how our work as therapists should be – a sacred recognition that what we are involved in is work of the greatest seriousness. That there is nothing more important than the atmosphere of healing, the *quality* which grows, through the work of both sides, in the coming together of the one who needs, and the one who can be honest about the information they have, and the belief they hold in the client's ability to repair what has been damaged, to face the truth, and find their way back to a fulfilling life.

Section Two

Overweight

CHAPTER EIGHT

Understanding
Overweight as a Disorder

If you are starting the book here it is important that you are aware of the style in which it is written. Some information is repeated.

You may not need to have this, but in my experience people with an eating disorder gain by hearing the same information repeated. Please overlook the repetition if it is not helpful to you.

The first time I presented my ideas to a group of client-centred counsellors and therapists one woman, who worked more with overweight people, asked if there was a way to apply my model to overweight (as you will note, I prefer the term 'overweight' to 'obesity'). At the time it took me by surprise, since I was thinking of eating disorders as pertaining only to underweight. Off the cuff I started to see if there were similarities and connections that could be made. But it has only been in the months since then that I have looked properly into the issue of overweight as also being subject to and motivated by an EDM.

According to Bidgood and Buckroyd (2005, p.221): 'Obesity has become a world-wide problem of epidemic proportions (World Health Organization, 1998). In England it has almost quadrupled in the past 25 years (United Kingdom House of Commons Health Committee, 2004) and now affects 25% of men and 20% of women (Great Britain Office for National Statistics, 2004). In spite of a flourishing slimming industry and widespread desire among all Western and westernised communities to achieve personal slimness, no headway is being made in reducing the prevalence of obesity. Research indicates that obese people can, with treatment, reduce their weight, but usually regain all of the weight lost over a period of five years at most (Wardle, 1999; Wilson & Brownell, 2002)'.

Further in the report the authors note probable causes: 'In most cases, the root cause of the participants' obesity was understood by them to lie in the environment of their childhood and adolescence, significant precursors to obesity being trauma, encouragement to overeat, lack of exercise, or rebellion against a perceived over-emphasis on weight control.... Some participants experienced a loss of control over eating, a craving for food at some stage of weight gain ... Many participants showed low self-esteem and lack of self-confidence and felt unattractive and depressed.' (Bidgood & Buckroyd, ibid, p. 227).

Of particular interest to me, in the light of developing the idea of some kind of actual eating disorder *mechanism*, is the comment above that 'some participants experienced a *loss of control* over eating, a *craving for food at some stage of weight gain'* (my italics). Could it be that this observation is describing the action of an EDM – an OEDM or Overweight Eating Disorder Mechanism?

The report includes quotes from the 18 participants of the authors' study:

'Participant: 'I really got to a panic point. You do feel panicky when you feel that you've got to have something to eat. You feel a kind of nervousness and, if you eat, it goes away....

'You feel nerves inside, that I've never had before, but it seems to be a certain point of fatness that you get to, like a crossover point. On this side, up to this weight everything's all right and you can control yourself, but after a certain weight it seems that something else takes over and it's very, very hard to control. And it does make you feel, although there's nothing there to make you feel nervous or anxious about, it's just something to do with inside. I don't know what it is.' (Bidgood & Buckroyd, ibid, p. 223).

When I read this, with a shock I realised that I might know what it is: *'on this side, up to this weight, everything's all right and you can control yourself, but after a certain weight it seems that something else takes over and it's very, very hard to control'* (my italics). Again, does this indicate the presence of an OEDM?

A second survey, Grant and Boersma (2005), notes the issue of control: 'Difficult mealtimes were characterised by control battles between parent and child, with 6 participants reporting this pattern. Several spoke of being forced to eat foods they didn't like, which escalated into a battle of wills. These control battles became internalised and food later became associated with control issues.

M6: 'I had to eat what was on my plate and I couldn't substitute. I didn't have the control over the portions and that became my non-control.'

P: 'How did you handle food control?'

M6: 'I rebelled – getting pleasure, gaining excess weight, eating quantities of food impulsively'. (Grant & Boersma, 2005, p.215).

The similarity with underweight, where there is also a 'battle of wills' between the person and an outside authority figure, is distinct. If this is an indication that there might be an OEDM, where does that take us? Since there are similarities between the above and the quotations from research I note in the first section, surely it means that part of understanding overweight is understanding that it is *something to be recovered from*. In other words, that although there is not the violence of bulimia, or the specific and upsetting physical appearance of anorexia – *overweight may be another kind of actual EDM*. Obviously that would have profound implications for the therapeutic treatment and recovery process.

The theme of overeating being a form of self-harm or violence is developed in the report. 'Six participants, approximately half of the sample, reported having been abused during childhood, supporting correlations in the literature between obesity and histories of child abuse. Two had been sexually abused by relatives and four reported physical or emotional abuse by parent.... Each participant who reported abuse expressed sadness, anger, rebellion and pain connected with their childhood experiences'. (Grant & Boersma, ibid, p. 215).

Can it be that overweight is merely on the other end of the eating disorders line, with similar causes and identical experiences, with the only difference being the way in which the disorder is expressed by the individual –or more truthfully the individual's EDM/OEDM?

Before it seems that I am taking too drastic an approach, it is wise to pause and think about all the *other* causes that may be included in overeating. These are obvious, ranging from availability – over-availability of food, to fast food and unhealthy life styles. Yet just as every thin person doesn't have what I am characterising as a full-blown disorder, and every person who vomits is not bulimic, can it be that there is a *certain proportion* of overweight people in the general population who are missing a complete diagnosis of their situation?

Recently I told someone who works tangentially with me that I was now working on eating disorders. His face grew grim. 'I see those programmes on kids in those places. I want to say *why don't you for god's sake eat something?'* Just as this person does not have a professional's understanding of the situation, so I am wondering whether the same is often said of overweight: 'Why doesn't he/she just stop eating so much?'

On holiday last year I stayed in a hotel that offered a lavish all-inclusive breakfast. My attention was taken by a European couple. They were both noticeably overweight and in the hottest weather wore dark, nondescript and concealing baggy clothes. It was their attitude to the food that interested me. They both took two full plates of food – fancy bread, toast, sweet rolls, cheese, meat, hard-boiled eggs and other items. They ate the food very deliberately, silently, with determination. There was no sense that they were *enjoying* it. More it was as though the buffet table was a task, a task not to be enjoyed but to be endured. Calories were to be put into the mouth and it was no good thinking otherwise.

Continuing this thought, it came to me that there was no *relationship* between the food and the people eating it. Food was a vehicle for something else. Food was there to be consumed in order that something *else* could take place. Could that something be the attempt to satisfy an inner mechanism, an OEDM?

Rather than answering directly, I'll move on to another example. This woman I knew briefly some 25 years ago. In appearance she was blonde, small and sizeable. The day I had tea with her she launched into detail about how 'the doctor tells me my weight is all about glands. My glands are the problem'. At the same time, within two hours, she opened and consumed the contents of two packets of biscuits.

Again there appeared to be no relationship between what she was putting in her mouth and the consequences. She was *aware* of being overweight, but had seized on 'glands' as an answer. Would it have helped her if, at the time, I had had the understanding that I am developing now? Could I have said something on the lines of: 'Have you been aware of the two packets of biscuits? If so, surely you have information about what *else* may be responsible for the weight? And if not, *what's the point* of eating – unless it's to satisfy this 'other' inside you?'

It may seem that there is a contradiction in the idea that overweight people have no relationship with food. Some would argue that that is the *only* thing they have a relationship with, using food as an emotional 'crutch', as compensation, for emotional support, etc. However I use relationship in the positive sense: something that supports and nurtures. Something that knows when enough is enough. So having a relationship with food really means having a healthy relationship. And a healthy relationship is one where you remember there is a life *beyond,* and bigger than, the food in front of you.

The existence of an OEDM would need to be taken into account in getting this new idea right. Just as I advocate *separation, negotiation* and *taking back* the energy of the underweight EDM, so in reversing the power of an OEDM we would need to do it with an awareness of *something else going on inside* – as seemingly noted in the observation of the participants previously given as an example.

To further explore this I looked back at my own days of being overweight. The first thing is to describe the density of dreams in which I lived. There was very little that broke through the state of non-awareness. One moment of clarity occurred, around 13, a couple of days after I had eaten a 200gm bar of chocolate and a family sized packet of crisps. I remember putting on shorts and couldn't fasten the button.

The momentary awareness was that it was because of the chocolate and the crisps. In other words, that there *was* a momentary, fragmentary understanding that the food going in and my body weight *did have a connection*. But then it was lost in waves of 'sleep' as I put on another, bigger, pair of shorts and forgot about it.

Only years later when I was motivated to begin losing weight did I begin to put the relationship between myself and food under the microscope. Had I *not* then become consumed by the awakening of the underweight EDM, I might have achieved my initial goal of losing weight and that would have been the end of it.

Professor Susie Orbach created a whole new understanding of approaching overweight with Fat is a Feminist Issue (1978). She notes (p. 18): 'A feminist perspective to the problem of women's compulsive eating is essential if we are to move on from the ineffective blame-the-victim approach and the unsatisfactory adjustment model of treatment. While psychoanalysis gives us useful tools to discover the deepest sources of emotional distress, feminism insists that those painful personal experiences derive from the social context into which female babies are born, and within which they develop to become adult women.

'The fact that compulsive eating is overwhelmingly a woman's problem suggests that it has something to do with being female in our society. Feminism argues that being fat represents an attempt to break free from society's sex stereotypes. Getting fat can thus be understood as a definite and purposeful act: it is a directed, conscious or unconscious, challenge to sex-role stereotyping and culturally defined experience of womanhood'.

Of course I was a fat boy child, not a girl child or adult woman. In my experience, and in the two examples I quote which *did* include adult women, it was much more a *lack of consciousness, a void in the relationship* with food. In my understanding, gaining weight is usually a by-product, let's call it, of OEDM activity. However, since I am also aware that victims of rape and sexual abuse say that they gained extra weight specifically so as not to appear sexually attractive clearly this is a situation with no simple answer.

As I will go on to detail in the next chapter, I have recently had the opportunity of working with a highly motivated, overweight woman. She has done all the diets, 'read all the books, lost a mountain of weight and gained it again'. How she has responded to my developing theory I believe makes an interesting addition to current thought on treatment and recovery in overweight.

As I also detail, my client immediately took to the concept of an OEDM. As she says: 'It's like I can't help myself. I *know* the food is wrong for me, but I just can't stop. I don't eat until I'm starving, and then I cram it into my mouth. I'm not eating, I'm *ramming* it down my throat. I *attack* my food' This description reminds me of the bulimic experience, as often related by a client: 'It's not that I *want* to throw up, sometimes, it's that there's something inside me driving me on. And there comes a moment when I realise I can't *not* throw up'.

I continue to ponder the psychic meaning of overweight. Perhaps it is a by-product of both a *lack* of relationship and an awakened OEDM. I'm thinking of the tiredness and lethargy that often accompany overweight. This need to escape, the hours spent in valueless daydreaming or fantasy seem to be *another manifestation of the moving centre*. Is it true, therefore, that just as underweight I believe to be located as a defence mechanism in the moving centre, that overweight is *also* in the moving centre – but here expressed as a *lack of movement?*

I remember for myself the paralysing fear of knowing I had to take part in the annual school two-mile cross-country run. Nowadays I would take part and enjoy it, then I would dread for weeks the agonising, approaching day. I remember the year I tried to give myself some extra energy by eating. Unfortunately I ate my usual comfort – crisps – and so not only did I have to run up hill but my throat was assaulted by a terrible, ragged thirst. Whatever was dictating my choice of food had *clearly* let me down – and doesn't that also sound like some sort of OEDM? Who in their right mind would eat crisps and not have a drink before a two-mile run – other than someone whose attitude towards food was being dictated by something inner *that was not equipped to do the job?*

Readers who are beginning on this chapter may feel the need to have the rhetorical question above answered. The answer is that I am coming to believe that it would be an OEDM – Overweight Eating Disorder Mechanism, just like that when the underweight EDM has woken up as a result of gaps in the person's psychic defences and now seeks to run their life and make their decisions in its own dangerous and unprofitable way.

Would not this explain the phenomenon of 'comfort food'? Where clear-headed thinking is called for, where action rather than hours of miserable inner questioning is required – only an OEDM would advise eating food as the answer to all ills – the way the underweight EDM advises only denial and exercise (in anorexia) and bingeing and purging (in bulimia).

So what we have come to see as a traditional method for coping with life's commonplace difficulties may in fact be something far more sinister: a shared lack of awareness that what is going on is having a severe, possibly disabling, effect on a person's ability to make an effective response to a *specific* situation.

The main headline of The Times newspaper for September 6, 2007, read: 'Food additives make children behave badly.' The lead story, (Elliot, 2007), stated 'Research for the Food Standards Agency and published in *The Lancet* has established the 'deleterious effects' of taking a mixture of artificial extras that are added to drinks, sweets and processed foods. It has led the FSA to issue the advice to parents who believe their children to be hyperactive that they should cut out foods containing the E numbers analysed in the study.

'After consuming the drinks – a cocktail of controversial E numbers and the preservative sodium benzoate – the children were found to become boistrous and lose concentration. They were unable to play with one toy or complete one task, and they engaged in unusually impulsive behaviour. The older group were unable to complete a 15-minute computer exercise' (p. 1).

What I found particularly interesting about the *effects* of the artificial foodstuff was the description of *disordered behaviour*. Extending the scope of the findings, I would like to suggest that these sorts of foods would appeal to a *disorder*, with the consequential manifestation of disordered behaviour.

However this is only a fragment, and I am not offering as a rational hypothesis. Only that I am setting it down because it might be useful to add to the mix.

More to the point, as noted in Body Images, Eating Disorders and Obesity in Youth (Smolak et al., 2001), is research into the children in America affected by food issues: 'The Heart, Lung and Blood Institute sampled 2379 black and white, 9 and 10 year old girls (Schreiber et al., 1996). Among 9 year old 42% of black and 37% of white reported that they were trying to lose weight; corresponding for 10 years old was 44% and 37%.

A second survey involved 'girls (5882) and boys (5585) in 9th to 12th grades (Serdula et al., 1993) Females trying to lose weight in percentages: white – 47.4, black – 30.4, Hispanic – 39.1, other racial identifications – 45.6.

'Males trying to lose weight in percentages: white – 16.2. black – 10, Hispanic - 16.7, other racial identifications - 13.7. (p. 1 & 2).

A third survey, by Field et al. (1999), involved 16,000 9 – 14, boys and girls of whom 93% were white. At 9 years, 20% and by 14, 44% had been on a diet. 4.2% of 13 year olds were always on a diet to lose weight while 11% exercised daily specifically to lose weight.

The book notes that 'ranges across a variety of different countries are quite consistent, indicating that round 30 – 50% of child and adolescent girls are weight-dissatisfied or dieting (Devaud, Jeannin, Narring, Ferron and Michaud, 1998, Lunner et al. 2000, Percemitre 1997, Sasson, Lewin & Roth 1995).

'In contrast to girls dissatisfaction, boys may be unhappy because they desire a larger and more masculine appearance (McCreary & Sasse 2000, Smolak, Levine & Thompson 2001) (Smolak et al, ibid, p. 2).

What does all this attention given to losing weight tell us? Possibly that, as has been noted in the underweight literature, practically *everyone* has a disordered relationship to food. Although only a percentage – a growing percentage – fall under the BMI requirement for a diagnosis of obese, it is a rare person who can truly claim to be entirely 'disorder free' – and the age at which a disordered pattern begins is getting younger and younger.

I am not saying that everyone who is, say, BMI classed as overweight has an eating disorder. I do, however, wonder if just as underweight has the category EDNOS – Eating Disorder Not Otherwise Specified – elements of a disorder may underpin overweight eating patterns.

In Fat, Loathing and Public Health (Austin, 1999) it is noted (p. 245) that 'the distinguishing pathology of eating disorders is obsessive concern with food, fat and diet, yet these characteristics are not abnormal in our culture, particularly for women'.

Complicating this basic statement, says the author, is a sense of confusion and wasted effort. The author also notes that public health literature focuses on *educating* overweight people to understand that what they are eating is bad for them. Whereas studies have shown that overweight people are *the most likely* to be sensitive towards overweight, and the most likely group to be informed about it.

Clearly it's not aggressive stares or unwelcome statements about 'fat' that will generate a connection between the situation of overweight, the desire to lose weight and maintain a weight loss, and the ability to fulfil that desire. But what if, just as with underweight, all along the presence of an *actual body mechanism* has been hampering the individual's goal? A mechanism that cannot even be blamed since it is trying to do its best to protect the individual and get them through another day.

It's interesting to note how, in Ameria, the advertisers and advertising agencies have made *hunger* something to *fear*. 'Don't forget to have one of our snacks between meals. *You have no idea when hunger will strike*' is the gist of some ads I came across. This is extraordinary. Somehow the copywriter has tapped into the opinion of the OEDM, that 'feeling hunger' is something sinister, perhaps even fatal.

The reality is food tastes better when you're feeling hungry, so you're robbing yourself of a real pleasure when you constantly feed yourself up, to avoid the 'dread hunger'. Does this have a parallel with 'nameless dread?' A slogan like *you have no idea when hunger will strike* is like any other advertising ploy. It does not necessarily need to have your best interests at heart: it's purpose is to sell product.

Therefore to have a sane and healthy relationship with food, food needs to be prized as necessary for human life, enjoyed for its own sake – and then not made to stand in for any other need or deprivation.

I remember a client saying to me that previously, when he wanted a treat, he would take three cakes, lock himself in his room, eat them – and then throw them up. 'But now' he said 'coming here (for therapy) is my treat'.

And that's a very sensible way to look at it. I remember discovering that exercise *wasn't* a nightmare. Recalling my school days, when I would do anything to avoid having to take part in the annual school run, the pleasure that I began to feel when I started running on my own initiative was quite extraordinary.

So, to paraphrase what my client was saying, discovering the pleasure of looking into himself in a supportive environment was as intense a pleasure as his acting-out.

And stopping over-eating is just as pleasurable because what the one hand gives up, the other hand receives in a different kind of plenty – one that encompasses everything else that life offers.

So far in this chapter I have begun an exploration into the concept of an OEDM. Now I would like to put together and further clarify my developing theories and understanding.

As I've just said, I don't think that every person with an overweight issue is harbouring a full-blown eating disorder, an OEDM. It is said that if we gain just one pound a year from the age of 20, at 60 we will be 40 pounds overweight. Such a weight gain would be seen as 'normal' – but someone else who is 40 pounds overweight may have an activated OEDM.

What working with my overweight client, as detailed in the next chapter, has suggested to me is that a disorder may be present *where there is a disparity between what the person could be, and how they are.* In other words, where *other* factors are maintaining an overweight situation, then it may be helpful to explore the ideas I am examining in this chapter.

So, to reiterate: just as with an EDM, an OEDM may be an actual mechanism, again most probably located in the *moving* centre, which wakens as a result of a number of factors in order to *protect and assist the individual.* Just as with an underweight EDM, the OEDM is not so much the lesser of two evils as the *greater.* The relationship an overweight person may have with food – 'comfort eating' or 'reward eating' – has parallels with underweight. Just as with an EDM, in an OEDM food is being used to create a dyadic relationship – the individual and their food – at the *expense* of a fully engaged relationship with the outside world.

Therefore there is the same massive resistance from the overweight person to the idea of taking off weight because it may psychologically leave them *naked.* Just as the EDM, with its very narrow boundaries and programmed, mechanical behavioural traits can only starve/exercise or binge/purge, so with an OEDM the person cuts themselves off from full human contact so as to 'enjoy' their relationship with food.

Therefore the process for gaining recovery from an OEDM is surely the same: separation, negotiation, a gradual exchange of 'closed and open hands' as the energy comes back from the OEDM into to healthy self.

Just as I am theorising that, with an EDM, you have the EDN – Eating Disorder Normal – that can only contract, not expand (so gently expanding the EDN is the key to recovery), so with the OEDM it's *contracting* the OEDN (Overweight Eating Disorder Normal) that needs to come on board.

That is because, as my client in the following chapter discovered, unless the OEDN is reduced and integrated into the NN —Normal Normal – then the OEDM will *continue* to regard the 'normal' as being the higher weight. But once the OEDN contracts until the point where it then becomes integrated as the new NN, then I am suggesting that *the new weight becomes the new NN, and the person may not return to the higher weight.*

At the moment this can be only a hypothesis. Unlike my exploration with underweight clients, I have only my own experience, my current theories, and one client in early therapy with which to back up these suggestions. I would expect that by the time I issue a second edition of this book I will have more concrete evidence, more results.

Pointers Towards Overweight Disorder

- You don't eat food because you enjoy it but because you can't not stuff yourself
- You build your day around food, meal by meal
- All events revolve around food and if you aren't able to eat you feel cheated
- You can't understand how other people can eat or not eat
- You plan ways in which you can eat more than your share
- You like to eat in private and organise things so you are alone
- You hide food – it's like a secret resource whenever you want it
- You don't eat, you attack your food
- You lose hours, afternoons, even days 'wallowing'
- In between wallowing you eat food – whatever is available
- You prefer cheap food because there's more of it. You're not going to enjoy it so what difference does it make?
- Sometimes you feel driven to eat and anything in your way is a major frustration and there's no time to waste
- You know the calorific content of everything
- You have tried to diet but find you get lost in the wallowing
- You have to settle for second best and this makes you depressed
- People don't see the you inside, instead they make fun of you
- People don't see how kind and sensitive you are
- You wish you could be like other people and only take what you need
- You give and like to get chocolates and sweets rather than flowers or wine
- You may drink a lot, but it's the food which really hits the spot
- Sometimes you see other people and wonder how they can live without a full-on relationship to food
- At times it feels like something else is making you eat
- You look in the mirror and you don't recognise yourself
- You think even if the rest of your life isn't working, at least food gives you meaning

- You hate sounding out of breath and try to pretend it's not you
- You wish diets helped
- You sometimes have such determination – but you've come to realise it goes and you can't trust yourself
- You wish you were really thin – that sounds like paradise

CHAPTER NINE

Case Study: Overweight 'The Lack of Relationship'

As always, names and details have been changed. Additionally the story is from more than one source.

Jenny is a pretty, dynamic, highly intelligent woman in her early 30s. She has peaches-and-cream skin, big blue eyes and an abundance of blonde hair. I'm sorry if this sounds like I'm reducing her to a to a purely physical description, but it's relevant for you to have a visual picture.

Let me introduce Jenny in her own words, describing a recent incident:

'In my job as an interior designer I have to speak to suppliers on a daily basis. For the last couple of months I've been having friendly and increasingly flirtatious chats with Andrew, a clerk at one curtain suppliers. When I mentioned, in one of our friendly chats, that I was coming up to Birmingham to inspect the new season's fabrics personally he immediately suggested we meet for lunch.

'Are you sure?' I asked?

'Positive' said Andrew. 'You don't have a bodybuilder boyfriend do you?'

'No boyfriend at all'.

'Terrific. I'm between ladies myself'.

'Do you want to see my photo first? I mean, what if you don't like what you see but I still need to source fabric?'

He laughed. 'No problem. I'd turn you over to Sharon! That's what I do with all my nuisance calls'.

Jenny hesitated. 'I have to warn you – I'm a big girl'.

Andrew laughed again. 'That's okay! I don't mind a bigger girl – size eight or even size ten'.

Jenny hesitated again. 'Uh, I think I'm more size 16'.

Jenny and Andrew exchange photos. Jenny was pleased with his, and looked forward to their next talk. She waited for his call. The next day she called to speak to Andrew – and got put through to Sharon. Since then Andrew has refused any contact with her.

Jenny related this incident calmly and with dignity. She acknowledged that it hurt – as did other situations with similar outcomes. She *also* used it as the bedrock, the foundation for a new inner determination *not to be treated like this ever again*.

Jenny and I had very quickly bonded. She has a warm and infectious personality coupled with a gentle and sensitive demeanour. She was not interested in accepting her weight and expecting people to love her for her inner person – she wanted what she saw others as having – 'first impressions wow factor'.

When she was very young she was separated from her parents in a shopping mall. The four hours it took to find her 'was an eternity for my parents'. She believes that as a direct result of this incident, forgotten by Jenny but still referred to by her parents, she grew up as something of 'a princess, swathed in cotton wool and spoiled beyond belief'.

Her father worked as a chef at a prominent hotel. Jenny recalled that if she complained about the meal at home he would immediately leave his own food to cook her whatever she desired. When she related this I said it was interesting because of the analytical theory that there are *two* main causes of what subsequently may manifest as an eating disorder: a mother unable or unwilling to contain the baby's emotions, or a mother or parents who *overindulge*, thereby inadvertently preventing the developing baby from finding for itself the ability to self-maintain, and tolerate frustration.

In terms of therapy goals, Jenny is specific: she wants to go back to at least a size 14: 'Until eighteen months ago I was a 14 and I felt myself. But then I ballooned to an 18 or 20. But now I appear to have stabilised at a 16, and it's too much'.

Another reason for coming to therapy is the man in Jenny's personal life. He is Barry, a married man who has told her he will never leave his wife and children. She has been trying to break up with him for a couple of months and although they both agree it's essential she has lacked the willpower or even the complete conviction to make the final break.

This, she says, is because of her sense of neediness: 'I tell myself he's not right for me but then when we've spent the weekend together (Barry's wife travels extensively on business) after he's gone I feel absolutely devastated. Then I head for the fridge or the nearest takeaway'.

One thing that immediately struck me about Jenny was her intelligence – 'although I'm the first to admit I'm dumb around men and emotions'. She has a Masters Degree in Art Appreciation. As she puts it: 'I can't settle for the men I can get. If they're not married, they're much older or they've got kids and don't want any more. I want a family of my own – I just think I can do better than the men who are attracted to me'.

So her initial goal was to find the strength to break up with Barry. She also wanted to be able to live on her own and like it – but she couldn't bear the sense of inner emptiness: 'I go home on Friday night with great ideas of what I'm going to do over the weekend. But by Saturday lunchtime I'm so desperately needy I can't think straight. If Barry's available I spend the rest of the time with him – often arguing – or I will find a female friend and hit a restaurant and a couple of bars. I just can't be alone at the weekend, it's too painful'.

I discussed with Jenny the idea of how, in the growing baby, it is believed that gaps develop in the psyche because of some lack or missing element in the nurturing routine. In her case it seems it was because she was never allowed to find self-sufficiency. So as an adult she experiences the psychic gaps as loneliness and neediness, gaps that she plugs with food.

It's well recognised in the sports and health world that exercise is beneficial not only in keeping the body toned but also that exercise produces chemicals that make us feel good. When we feel good we don't need the calorie stimulation of too much food, so we naturally eat less. I recalled to Jenny that Lavinia, a woman in Mexico who approached me through my website, once wrote that she uses food 'in those little moments when nothing else is happening' – in other words, to plug a gap.

I also talked about the FIRO-B diagnostic tool. The letters stand for Fundamental Interpersonal Relations Orientation – Behaviour. It was developed during World War 2, to clarify whether seamen in submarines were compatible with their environment. One of the three aspects it measures is the *scale of need to express and receive affection.*

Obviously regarding the seamen, 'affection' is understood in terms of literally not rocking the boat. I mentioned that when I took the test a few years ago, I was an 8 on the scale of need to express affection (this translates well into my being a therapist, since I see the world in terms of how I can be helpful!). Jenny, immediately grasped its significance. On a scale of 0 to 9, 'I feel I'm a 9 on the *need to receive affection*'.

This was helpful in beginning to sort out the confusion and clouds in her head, and giving basic concepts she could hang some understanding on. I mentioned also the book *Women Who Love Too Much*. Jenny said she immediately identified with the title. Jenny also said that when she was with Barry, or any man she was dating at the time, *her need for more than necessary food went away.*

We pondered whether generally a high need to express and/or receive affection, which naturally had advantages in a supportive relationship, when in an unsatisfactory relationship resulted in an ongoing state of emotional neediness. *And* what part having emotional needs fulfilled by a romantic relationship played in controlling, reducing the need or substituting for food.

Jenny got excited. For the first time, rather than seeing *no relationship* between food, herself and her emotional neediness, she could see that in fact it was an interlocked triangle. Therefore, by loving herself she could fill up the psychic gaps, thereby reducing her neediness and making food as a substitute for affection less necessary.

The next session Jenny shared a particular insight. On one of the evenings since we had last met she had experienced a deep sense of contentment which she had said she wanted to find but never thought she could. It happened the day after our previous meeting.

'It's not that I didn't know it before, but now I have something solid to work from, now I can do something about it'.

During this session we decided the next one would take place at 7am! This was my suggestion, prompted by Jenny saying that she so loved the early hours of the day, but knew she wasted them 'wallowing in bed'. I commented that 'wallowing' seemed to be appropriate for the OEDM – being a disorder, it felt secure in, and promoted, disordered conditions. It had been a few years since I'd had a 7am session, but I thought it would help re-enforce Jenny's new found determination.

By Jenny challenging herself to get up, out and in my therapy room by 7am, she was starting to change her whole way of thinking and working. Because Jenny relishes the early hours, she got excited about being able to do things other than wallow – read, watch TV, plan the day. I commented that the difference would be that this would be an *active* process – which would make the OEDM passive. Just as with the EDM, when the person is active the OEDM cannot rush in to fill up gaps with its negative manifestation.

The 7am idea worked well. Jenny arrived already in make-up and primed for a dynamic session. Something interesting I noticed in passing was that when I opened the door to her there was a difference in what I could term her *physical aura*. What I mean here is when Jenny first came to sessions she came to discuss emotional neediness, not her relationship to food. But when I first saw her it was as though she was whispering: 'Food – I am a big person'. But now even her *aura* seemed to be changing, gearing up to take her into new territory. In fact she was already losing weight – 2kg as weighed on the gym scales.

In this session we looked at the curious incongruity between Jenny as a person, and her relationship to food and overweight. She has a master's degree and a great career and is rightly offended that the men she wants don't want her, as she sees it, only because of her weight. What she is doing in therapy is bringing her intelligence and her weight *into alignment*.

As always when one writes about someone's desire to lose weight it needs to be couched in appropriate terms. I do not function as a 'diet doctor' or nutritionalist. I respond only to what is important to my client, and with Jenny she was clear that taking off weight was crucial to the goals she had.

At the 7am meeting I presented Jenny with my thinking around the OEDM. That I was coming to believe that an OEDM maintains a person's overweight at a constant level. This is why, when people diet, once they have gone through the active phase of losing weight, they are most often not able to maintain it – most weight is put back within five years. There is an explanation to be found for this if we consider the idea that the *OEDN – Overweight Eating Disorder Normal* - is still stuck at the higher weight. Therefore, just as with the EDN the idea is to *expand* what it will tolerate – the two silhouettes concept – so with overweight we require the OEDN to *contract*, so that once weight loss is achieved the OEDN contracts to it, eventually becoming the new NN – Normal Normal.

I have had to understand what I believe is happening on the underweight side of the line before I could extend this to include the overweight end. But the fundamental principal remains the same. By becoming active it makes the OEDM passive, and this begins the weight reduction process. 'Wallowing' is the OEDM's way of keeping the person in a prison of sleep, like living in a cloud, wafting in and out of consciousness. This may be what people are trying to express when they say: 'I'd love to diet but I don't have the willpower' – the energy is in the OEDM, and the OEDM is using it to maintain its manifestations through wallowing, disordered food situations and using food as a substitute for other aspects of living.

As previously noted, research as far back as the 1970s in America showed that of all the different groups, people who were overweight were the ones who knew most about dieting and exercise. Which was why, the report maintained, the concept of using financial resources to *educate* overweight people was a waste of money and resources. Could it be that what was really needed was an understanding of the presence of an OEDM, something that got in the way of overweight people's knowledge, dragging them back into the spiral of wallowing, over-eating and depression?

We again agreed to meet at 7am the following week. My notes said: 'I'm not mad about this extra effort on my part, but I am pleased to encourage Jenny'. Reflecting, I thought that our process needed to be gradual, something Jenny would be able to manage on an ongoing basis, gently reducing the perimeters of her OEDN, gradually introducing healthier attitudes and use of her time. As with the EDM, we did not want to antagonise an OEDM, which if it existed had come into existence as a defence and support for Jenny at the time.

Our next early morning session was scheduled for Thursday, but since Jenny was attending twice-weekly, the next time we met was on Tuesday evening. She surprised me by saying she had spent the weekend with Barry – they had gone to Norfolk for 'a goodbye weekend'. I was somewhat stunned. I said the idea was somewhat unusual, since when people wish to break up, spending a romantic weekend together might not be the most sensible approach.

She said she felt very confused. The intimacy they had shared over the weekend meant that when she returned to her own flat her sense of neediness skyrocketed. And she began to obsess about food. On Monday she had been able to push these thoughts away, but earlier in the day we were meeting she had eaten black beans for lunch with chicken.

Here there were two issues. Firstly that she noted the relationship between the void and filling it with food, and secondly that she hadn't, for example, stuffed herself with cake – her choice of food had been within appropriate boundaries. She relaxed when I offered this and I said we were not trying to get her to think of all food as unacceptable – *that* would be finding ourselves in anorexic territory. In fact it might have been that something *healthy* inside her had been telling her that that was what she needed – good carbohydrate and protein.

However she also noted that she was finding *whatever* food she ate much more tasty and she looked forward to it with much greater relish than she had been used to previously. I responded that this could also be two things: when people diet or restrict their food intake, then whatever they do eat has a bigger impact on the system. Vegetarians often maintain that they don't miss meat because, without meat, 'veggies taste much better'. Alternatively, and more sinisterly, it could be the OEDM fighting back, wanting to maximise the pleasure of food in the hope that Jenny would return to a more disordered eating pattern. So we reserved judgement on the development until we could understand it better.

In this session Jenny also said that she had fallen somewhat on her exercise schedule. I responded that this was only to be expected. When we begin something it comes with a great deal of energy. But with repetition the energy wanes. What is most important was to find an overall determination, and re-find it when it got lost. It wasn't about success or failure – both of which can cause the OEDM to get involved – but bringing about a shift. For example, she was still walking to work in the morning, and that gentle exercise was consistently challenging the old 'wallowing'. It is, of course, also crucial that the person does not expect too much from themselves – the instillation of hope is much more helpful than creating an overly demanding regimen which quickly overwhelms.

Having struggled, after being frequently disturbed in the night by external noise, to be ready at 7am on Thursday for our next session I was disappointed to get a text from Jenny saying she had been unable to sleep and couldn't make the session. We re-fixed it for 7pm the same day. When she arrived for the evening session she seemed upset, almost ashamed.

I put the situation in context by suggesting that it would be unrealistic to think that just because she had suddenly decided on an ordered existence, all the disorder would instantaneously fall into place. The OEDM was fighting back. We would both need to understand this.

In this session Jenny offered an observation that really excited me, since it seemed to be proof of the existence of an OEDM. Jenny had enjoyed a lunch with noodles. Then one of the design assistants had been going to the shop and before she could stop herself Jenny ordered a bar of chocolate. At the time she thought 'why not?' but she also knew she had planned to go to the gym in the evening, and the one would cancel the other.

Jenny related that she hardly noticed while she was eating the bar of chocolate. It was only the last couple of mouthfuls that she could recall enjoying. She said she had definitely not been hungry, but had ordered the chocolate because – well, something had not been able to resist.

The fact that she hadn't even enjoyed eating it seemed to imply that her taste buds hadn't been involved. Just as with an EDM, where the mechanism mechanically over-reacts to food and blindly denies it, so with an OEDM it's not about pleasure, but the OEDM *manifesting itself*. I recalled to her the incident I had observed on holiday in Egypt. How the couple at breakfast had mechanically chewed their way through piles of food without seeming to enjoy any of it. Enjoyment wasn't the point – the OEDM filled up a gap with its own solution to situations – to eat.

Jenny responded positively to the idea of the OEDM's manifestation. I said that, unlike with an underweight situation where someone might, in extreme circumstances, die from the illness, there is a lot less pressure on someone who is overweight to be meticulous about their intake. But in fact it's the same situation. Therefore the same approach may effect a cure: rather than allow everything to just pile on through the mouth, Jenny would be helped by getting as sensitive towards the food that goes in as I was when I was having to get my relationship with my own EDM absolutely right so I could recover, a little, day by day.

Here again I cautioned her. It might be that the OEDM really is just a different manifestation on the same line as the EDM. Therefore although getting more sensitive to what she ate was good in overcoming the OEDM's desire to manifest itself in inappropriate food intake, she did not want to inadvertently become so preoccupied with what she ate that an underweight EDM would become engaged in order to 'help' her screen out food.

Here I will also note similarities between the EDM and an OEDM. Both appear to be activated in response to holes in the person's psyche which have appeared for any number of reasons. Both seek to use food as a means of filling the holes, either through denial or through over-emphasis. Both seem to involve their own concept of how the body should be, either at an overweight level, or underweight. And both can be worked with by the person becoming active, since neither the OEDM or the EDM 'has a plan'.

It follows that the action of an OEDM has never been recognised. People who begin to take off weight *frighten the OEDM* – which like the EDM is a mechanism with an animal-like brain – and that fright causes the person to believe they need to drop the idea of losing weight.

Jenny noted that she was still very focussed on her food. Without the support of our sessions she may have been too vulnerable and confused by this to maintain her determination to lose weight. This needs to be understood within the context of what had been going on for years, that Jenny's OEDM was deliberately intervening in the relationship Jenny wished to have with food by creating a disordered food pattern and thereby 'helping' her fill the inner holes.

Jenny also talked about how she eats: 'I attack food'. This was interesting for the similarity it bears with bulimia, in that both are to do with *violence*. Obviously having a savage relationship to food is something that would nourish a disorder. Therefore the way to recover would be something gentle, something that doesn't feed the mechanism. Something that, being outside of the sphere of influence of the OEDM, would necessarily come from the *healthy* part of the person.

At our next session Jenny surprised me by asking if it had been difficult for me to learn 'all the jargon'. That I must have done a lot of reading to understand all the concepts – OEDM, OEDN, NN etc. I said no, all of these concepts were my *original* thinking – and that she was the first person to hear about them. As I said this I wondered how it might sound but she, as always, took this information well. 'I'm not going to think about what this might mean. I don't want to get overwhelmed by some sort of pressure to get it all right. I'm just going to carry on regardless!'

Jenny was aware that she needed a lot of reinforcement since she sometimes felt the pressure of her OEDM left her no space to think and behave as she would prefer. An example of this reinforcement came from an unexpected quarter. She was filling time before meeting friends by having a solitary coffee in one of Soho's glamorous watering holes. She became fascinated by the reflections in a wall of mirrors. Suddenly she became aware of a handsome man, in reality sitting some distance away, but reflected up close. He was staring at her in a way unmistakable – 'we're talking intense lust!'

Jenny noted that basically what the man could see were her eyes and her blonde hair. I wondered if in fact he could see more of her, and liked what he could see. No, she was adamant, all he could see were her eyes and blonde hair. She stared back at him, hoping he wouldn't spoil it by rising from his chair and coming to find her. Instead he continued to stare at her, and she bathed in his ardent admiration.

'When I left I didn't look back. But for a few minutes I experienced what it would be like to have *exactly* the man I want!'

We laughed, we agreed that she was being inordinately shallow – but I have come to believe that what works is what works – and the incident clearly worked for Jenny. Rather than some abstract idea of her prince charming, from then she worked with a new focus. 'Perhaps one day I'll go back there and he won't need to look in the mirror any longer ...'.

On a more practical level, Jenny also discovered that her high need 'to receive affection' meant pumping her day full of inspiring images. She began subscribing to magazines about health and fitness and cut out shapes to stick around her mirror. It reminded me of the notes I used to leave for myself. When I told Jenny this she said what she liked about it was the reminder that she had put those images up for *a reason* – to reinforce her sometimes ambivalent feelings about her self-project.

As we continued to work there were sessions where she would arrive with no make-up, her hair hastily tied in a top knot. 'I know what I want but today I just can't connect with it' she said one morning. 'Today I just don't have the push. I want to wallow. There's something so deep inside me that is crying out for oblivion'. She related an incident at her local supermarket. She had been standing at the checkout counter when a woman had pushed by with her trolley almost bursting with food for a party.

Jenny had looked at her sensible purchases and a great wave of desire washed over her. She put down her basket, unhooked a full size trolley, and for the next twenty minutes she roamed the aisles, filling her trolley with all the purchases she had been denying herself. However, when she had finished and was again standing at the checkout counter her eye caught a row of magazines. On the cover of one was the same model who appeared in one of the images around her mirror.

'So help me my whole evening went to pieces. For the next half hour it seemed like I went round the supermarket returning each and every item from my trolley. I hope they don't have cctv or they'll never let me back there. At the end I went looking for my own little basket and found someone had put some of their unwanted stuff in it. For a moment I considered buying it anyway, but since it was mainly guy's stuff like shaving cream I was able to resist!'

This novel way of satisfying a craving, or acting out a craving until another, healthier part can come through to save the day, should not be put into practice in a supermarket near you. But as we discussed in the session, it was a good example of how fragile the hold on a better purpose can be – and again how, even in the grip of an OEDM, if something else comes along you may have enough energy to again reverse the advice of the greedy internal mechanical voice.

One day about ten weeks into our sessions Jenny stood on her usual scales and discovered she had lost six kilos. She also reported, gleefully, that she had needed to make an emergency stop at Oxfam for a pair of trousers that would fit her properly. Although she had had periods in the past where she had been able to lose weight, at those times she had not had a structure for maintaining the weight loss. But now she felt more confident that she would have a response when the voice of the OEDN, the 'disorder normal' I believe exists, would insist that she was dangerously underweight, and needed to abandon her regimen.

Jenny also met up with Barry. He said he had had great news for her. She wondered if that meant he was leaving his wife. Apparently what it meant was the wife was going to visit her mother in America and would be gone for six weeks. At that point Jenny held up her hand to interrupt Barry's nervous, bright, chatter. 'I'm curious. You haven't said anything about how I look'. 'Actually', Barry replied, 'I saw you walking in the street yesterday. I can see a real difference! In fact that's when I got the idea to call'.

Jenny reported this in a dry tone. 'I didn't want to hurt Barry. So I didn't rub it in. In fact we carried on talking and then I said I had to go and I never gave him a reply. I was just so warm and breathless and sexy I left him to pay the bill and wafted out and into the night!'

As well as highlights Jenny acknowledged the moments that were continuing to be difficult. What she found helped was to go back to the idea of the OEDN. Not to keep relentlessly pushing herself towards a monotonous goal of losing weight and firming up, but to understand that inside her, mechanical parts of her were attempting to adjust to the changes and sometimes they rebelled. She found that taking time in the morning to think through what she was doing, 'always catching up with myself' helped to keep a balance as well as making a gradual weight loss achievable.

This was helpful for me to hear. Just as, with underweight, it is better to only gradually seek to replace weight, so that the EDM didn't become traumatised and kick viciously back, so with overweight keeping the weight loss as *secondary* to *psychological weight adjustment* made for a more healthy reduction. In this way Jenny could avoid any manifestation of an underweight EDM becoming involved.

Four months into our work together, seven and a half kilos lighter, Jenny took time to review what had happened. 'Sometimes

I wake up and I can't believe I am over a stone lighter. Then I panic, I feel like I lose my way for a moment. That's when it helps to remember some of the theory. It fills up the hole so the OEDM doesn't fill it'.

'I don't want to fill my whole day, my whole life, with this goal of reducing. I want to spread my energy into all sorts of areas. I want to find someone who will support the me I can see at times. And also I don't know what I want. But that doesn't frighten me as much as it used to. It's like I've got a new structure inside, or a new group of friends. It's an incredible feeling to realise I'm not stuck as I was. What I do with that depends on factors I can and can't control. At least I feel, now, I've got the same chances as other people'.

Section Three

Underweight and Overweight
The DIY Recovery Method

CHAPTER TEN

Underweight
The DIY Method

Although my method, naturally, focuses on the power of the individual to effect their own recovery, this doesn't mean it has to be in isolation. In fact, just the opposite. It is very important, if you are someone with an eating disorder, that you reach out for understanding and support. Just as with sexual abuse or violence, the disorder thrives in isolation and silence so a simple explanation to the right person will help break down the internal prison.

You could also make contact with beat, the eating disorders association, and perhaps find a counsellor or therapist who will understand where you are and what you are trying to accomplish.

To return to the premise of this book: it can be read by a professional in the field of eating disorders recovery. Or someone who is close to someone with a disorder. Or by someone who has a disorder – and who, like myself during my anorexic period, has no one else to help them.

In this and the next chapter I would like to offer my way to reach and disengage with the EDM, to recover and to find a life beyond the disorder. These two chapters sum up the rest of the book and lay out the most important aspects as well as giving simple thoughts and strategies for recovery. These can be used on their own if there is no other form of support, or in conjunction with medical, therapeutic or other sources.

One caveat: the seemingly simple text that follows makes more sense if you read it after having read the rest of the book. Only then will the key words and ideas convey their full meaning.

Let's begin where the book began: what is an eating disorder? It is a defence mechanism of the body that has gone terribly wrong.

How do we recover? By realising this – and then by separating from it. Think of David and Goliath – you are David and the disorder is Goliath. But using the proper strategy, David triumphed. The proper strategy is to do a little, day by day, to disengage the mechanism and allow the right centre in your body – the intellectual, the emotional, the moving (physical movements) or the instinctive (unconscious processes like breathing) - to take back the running of your own life.

The disorder is based in the *moving* centre. That's why the action of the disorder is a movement:

In anorexia, exercising and denying food.

In bulimia, bingeing and purging.

Obviously these are simplified statements of how your disorder may be operating. The important thing is to understand that *you* are *not* your disorder. *It* is a function of the body's defences, rooted in the moving centre, that has gone wrong.

Remember the image of the closed and opening hands. The exchange of these is best done in a gentle, gradual movement. The disorder is inside – therefore it can't be cut out, it can't be demolished. But it can be re-integrated.

It is essential that we have a *plan*. The disorder most probably has come about because of a combination of a lack of internal psychic and emotional resources, plus intolerable conflict. It may have been triggered off by sensitivity about weight, or childhood trauma. It may just be that you are frozen in adolescence or at any other stage of your life, and rather than progressing naturally, your psychic development has taken a wrong turn.

That wrong turn has caused the EDM – eating disorder mechanism – to wake up and try to live your life for you. That's why, at the beginning, it can feel like a good thing. Rather than feeling the pain of some situation, or having doubt or fear, the disorder encourages you to allow it to get stronger, using the energy from all your centres.

Then it is stronger than you, and just like the story of the Sorcerer's Apprentice – where the broomstick brought magically to life can only re-fill and re-fill buckets of water long after the action is meaningful or helpful - all the EDM can do, in answer to all of life's complexities and difficulties, is to cause you to either exercise and constantly diet, or to binge and purge.

Recognise that it will take you some time to recover. Think of it as you have somehow painted your house black. Re-painting it white will take time, and careful effort.

You have a particular help on your side, because when you become *active* it makes the disorder *passive*. Remember that if you don't have a plan, there will be a psychic space, a little void – and the disorder is programmed to rush in and fill up that space for you – but in its way, not yours.

So begin each day with a *plan*. You could start by writing out that famous 1960s slogan: 'Today is the first day of the rest of my life'.

And believe it because it's true. Every morning when you wake the day stretches out before you. It may be that you have come to dread that first thought in the morning, because you know the disorder will be refreshed and powerful. Therefore have a *plan*.

Rather than living your life from day to day, begin your life the night before. Make a plan at the end of the day, just for the next 24 hours. You could write your plan down – keeping a personal diary is an excellent way of, in a way, being *your own therapist*.

So inside your diary, write what you plan to eat the next day. Nothing too demanding, you don't want to distress the disorder.

But, each day that you can, do just a little more – remember always to negotiate with the disorder, to explain that you *need* the *fuel* in order to look after yourself, to work, to exercise. Focus on understanding what your disorder is about, and where you can have a say in things.

Remember the idea of the silhouette – growing the idea of 'normal'. That the original silhouette is how the disorder likes to think of your body – extremely thin. Now think that when you take in new food it creates a layer that surrounds the original layer. That the disorder *doesn't* like – so when you take in food, the disorder wants you to exercise or purge – in some way to get rid of that 'second layer'.

Your task, by gradual, small steps, is to find out how you can make the second silhouette *the normal*. The disorder began with you in one situation, at one weight – and gradually the 'normal' became less and less. So now you need to reverse the process, gently, day by day, adding a little more food gradually so the disorder's sense of 'normal' can adjust without it becoming negative. Recovery is partly an *experiment* to see what works – so if you get it wrong with too much food, don't despair, just calmly, the next day, start again.

Normal weight bulimics may appear to be no different to other people – but internally there's a sense of what is and is not acceptable. Internally the sense of 'normal' is like a clean sheet of paper on which food is dropped. The normal for the EDM is to purge the body of that food – so your task is to get the EDM used to the feeling of a little food in the body. Again do this gradually, and if and when you have a relapse, don't place too much importance on it, which really serves the cause of the disorder. Calmly begin the next day again.

Your work, each day that you can, is to add just a little more, so that gradually your *normal* increases, with the disorder not becoming alarmed or anxious. Remember that the disorder is a tyrant – but it is also very frightened. Reassure your disorder, all the while being aware of the necessity of taking energy back from it. By reassuring your disorder, by calming the beast, you are getting control over it.

As you find you are able in little steps to take back power, it will give you a greater sense of *confidence* and *trust* in yourself. This is very important. The disorder has increased its influence by keeping you confused and by your not having faith or confidence in yourself. Often that has come because growing up either you were not valued as a separate individual, or because your mother or parental figure did not allow you to develop your own defences, instead someone else was always there, helping you out. That may have left you weak and lacking a sense of your own power, or ability to look after yourself.

By taking control of yourself using my approach, you will have many, many opportunities to prove to yourself that you *can* make decisions, that you *can* be reliable – and that you can rely on yourself.

I like to think it will help if you keep reading this book. Try to read a little each day, particularly before going to sleep, so that each evening the words are able to grow in your mind. They are a source of *nourishment* for the psyche. This will also encourage your *instinctive* and *emotional* centres to start working again for you.

That will mean that you should expect to move in and out of different *subjective states*. Think of these states as comparable to the sort of internal shift people take drugs to experience. When you have starved or purged your body, any food coming in creates a great world of response in your exhausted and starving mind.

I'm not advocating getting a disorder as a way of experiencing 'druggie states'. But just to make the parallel that you can *expect* your mind, your whole body, to feel 'strange' or 'weird' when you start putting more food into it. So make a note to yourself: 'Feeling weird is only natural. More energy means my brain and my emotions are waking up'

Or whatever helps you. As always, use this book to empower yourself to come up with the thoughts and understandings that help you to always, a little at a time, detach from the disorder, and grow the healthy 'you'.

Don't shy away from acknowledging violence – in all its forms. Violence towards you, physical, mental or emotional, may be part of your history. It might seem that what's life is about. Don't let what hurt you before keep hurting you. A violent attitude towards yourself may have *fear* at its basis – fear of a dark void that opens up if you *stop* acting out the violence.

That will be part of your EDM. Separate from it, begin to understand how the EDM is working to keep you disordered, to keep it strong. The first step, in moving beyond bulimia, is to exchange the anger and whatever else you are carrying towards yourself with compassion. For hate, understanding. For past wrongs, an emotional letting go – and a new beginning.

Although you may believe that you have irreparably damaged your internal organs, that too could be part of the EDM's hold. Often when someone who has had an eating disorder has a thorough medical examination it is much more the psychic wound that becomes exposed. And the psychic wound is something that you are in the best position to heal.

Try to work with more positive images. If the world up till now seems full of pain, fear and violence, deliberately seek out a new set of images. Rather than watching a violent TV drama – watch programmes on the natural world. Rather than another evening cooped up in your room, take a walk and even if you have to hop on a bus – go somewhere that's a green, open space.

And when you're sitting surrounded by quiet and nature, consciously take *that* into your heart. Use nature to heal your wounds. Use silence, rest and the most basic human desire for inner peace to grow a calmer interior world. Stop allowing the cycle of a disorder to continue. Yes, it will take time and effort – but there was a time when you *were* able to take in food and get on with the rest of your life – if you can't go forward, go back and re-discover an easier, quieter time. As it says in the Desiderata *'strive* to be happy'.

One way in which you are more fortunate than I was when I had my disorder is that nowadays there are many more facilities and sources of help. A good nutritionist is a great help in thinking constructively about food – and you can show them this book if you feel it will help.

A sympathetic GP can also be a great help. You might want to talk about taking an anti-depressant just to give you a little help in taking the first steps. This is entirely up to you. Remembering my client's experience, for a long time he did without 'the little green pill' because he was fearful of the result. But when he started he felt relief from his un-resolvable internal conflict – and he was able to think more clearly and concentrate on his recovery.

You may find that you have cut off from friends, peers and those who love you because they don't understand. Showing them this book, or making some notes that make sense to you, might help. Your illness has affected those around you, and they may be wary or in despair about what can be done. Assure them that you are taking the first steps and seek to re-integrate yourself back in the world you left when you turned inward and into the world of the EDM.

If you have been used to visiting 'pro-ana' and 'pro-mia' internet sites you may find that anything you want to say about 'recovery' on them then brings you into conflict there. Recognise that when people write about the illness in a positive way they are under the influence of the illness, and so anything you say they will react against. Try to separate from that world and re-grow yourself in the wider, healthier world.

Don't hold yourself back by wanting acceptance from the *wrong* sort of peer group.

I have been right where you are and until I realised I was very ill I was 'happy'. But afterwards I looked back at how I had been living my life – isolated, buried in exercise, getting nowhere, entirely dependent on my family – and realised it had been a very subtle prison.

You, like I, hold the key to that prison. Not just the book you're reading, but that part of you which understands that the illness is something that you *can* find a way to cure yourself.

I say to my clients that, once they have recovered, the journey they have taken will have showed them a part of life that most people never see. In this way, even having the illness – and especially recovering from it – can be a terribly important growth episode in your life.

I can say that when I came back from the illness, I came back to life with an energy and a joy that has not left me. I still wake up each morning delighted that I have hours, and energy, and a brand new day.

Take heart. Take care. A final word of Eastern wisdom is that the one who is best qualified to show you the way is someone who has already walked that path. I walked the path of having an eating disorder, and now my life is focused on helping other people find their own way back.

Reading this book means you can no longer be the person you were when you started the book. It means that now you may understand what didn't make sense before. Now it's in your hands, to take a little step every day, to take your life back into your own control – to really understand the philosophy of 'Eating Disorder Self-Cure'.

One final thought. There may be times when you feel so alone you feel as though no one in the world knows what you are going through. But that's not right. There *is* somebody inside who listens. There is someone who has been witness to what has happened to you.

And that someone wants to help you now. Allow that to happen. That someone is your instinct to live. It is what has caused people through the ages to make super-human efforts. It has guided people faced with seemingly impossible odds. Your instinct to live will help you. Have faith. Have courage. Have hope.

CHAPTER ELEVEN

Overweight
The D-I-Y Cure

If you are beginning the book at this chapter, let me repeat the introduction from the previous chapter. In this chapter you will find, in simple form, the various ideas I have enlarged on in the second section, on Overweight, in this book. This chapter is intended to be a quick way of accessing the nub of the various ideas. It works best when you have read the other chapters on overweight. Since much of what is relevant to overweight is also relevant to underweight, reading the whole book will give you a complete understanding of my method.

I began writing about eating disorders only from the point of view of 'underweight'. But through working with someone with an overweight issue, and thinking through my own experience of being overweight, I have come to believe that much of what is relevant to underweight is also relevant to overweight.

In both circumstances, from my own experience and from what my clients with eating disorders have told me, I have come to believe that there may be an EDM – an Eating Disorder Mechanism – which in the case of overweight I call the OEDM.

As the name suggests this is a *mechanical* device, a defence mechanism in the body. I believe it is located in the *moving centre* – that is, the part of our self which controls our physical movements.

The reason I call it a *defence mechanism* is that I also believe that at the beginning, the OEDM is activated for a good reason. To understand this we have to go back to the early days of a baby's life.

Melanie Klein, Wilfred Bion and other psychoanalysts have looked deeply into the first couple of years of the baby's life. A number of different phases or states of development need to take place so that the baby becomes equipped with a full set of psychic defences.

Where this does not happen, it is my belief that there exist *psychic holes* or *a void* in the psyche. And, as the baby becomes a child, the child an adolescent and the adolescent an adult, in order to cope with life's pressures the OEDM is activated.

Like the EDM, in underweight, the OEDM is a different centre of control, an internal 'voice' which interferes with the normal running of things. Rather than leave the individual with the psychic gaps or void, the OEDM fills up the space by manifesting.

This movement is a drive towards food. It is known that the act of chewing switches off the brain – this is why chewing gum can fill up a boring moment and some people feel they can't function without chewing gum. The action of chewing clearly has a big meaning for the psyche.

With overweight, one aspect is the action of the OEDM using food to fill up the holes in an individual's life. The other aspect is that the OEDM gets in the way of the individual's *relationship with their food* – instead making it a *relationship with the OEDM*.

This, in my developing understanding, is why diets don't work. They *don't engage the OEDM*. Therefore the way to approach weight loss is similar to with underweight – it needs to be *negotiated with*.

By negotiating with the OEDM, you 'keep it on board'. The importance here is that without keeping your inner voice aware and calm about what is going on, it will strike back. Remember that it is a *defence mechanism*, which began with a good reason – to help the individual get through their life.

So by realising that it is inside, but not trying to be destructive, we start to have a different understanding of what is needed, psychically, to lose and *maintain weight loss*.

Therefore it may not be enough to just join a gym and cut out sugar – if you can even do that much. What is needed is to understand the need to recognise the existence of the OEDM, to separate from it, and negotiate with it.

Negotiate how? Remember that the OEDM is trying to keep you safe and emotionally separated from the world – and using food to do so. The problem is that, by using food, the overweight actually *attracts attention* – as well as being unhealthy etc.

I also believe that part of the OEDM is the OED*N* – *the Overweight Eating Disorder Normal*. This is another crucial piece of the puzzle. In underweight, what is needed is for the EDN – Eating Disorder Normal – to *expand*. In this way the person is able to eat a little more, and gradually get the EDN used to the presence of a little more food in the body.

With overweight, the idea is to *reduce* the OEDN until the individual has achieved their most 'normal' weight – the NN (Normal Normal as opposed to Overweight Eating Disorder Normal). This is crucial to counteract the longer term effect of the OEDN – which is to eventually *return the individual to their original weight, where the OEDN is set*.

However once you understand the concept of the OEDM and the OEDN it gives you fresh insight into the psyche. This can then be applied to weight loss. As the weight begins to come off, it can be expected that the OEDM will fight back. This can take the form of increased anxiety, or a sudden rush of interest in the food that is still eaten. You can also expect to suddenly find yourself acting in old ways – buying and consuming a bar of chocolate without being aware of what you're doing, for example.

The important thing here is that when you are *active* it makes the OEDM *passive*. This has also been remarked on in 'underweight' – the mechanical defence *does not have a plan*. But *you* can and should have a plan.

Start the *previous evening* to plan what you will be doing the following day. This means that when you wake up you already have the first thought – perhaps it's to wake up early enough to walk to work, or do some exercise. In this way you start off the day *actively* which makes the OEDM *passive* temporarily and allows a little energy to move from the OEDM back into the healthy body.

A client of mine referred to 'attacking' food. This is very interesting – what is your attitude to food? Is it the reward for work? The highlight of the day? Or do you eat mechanically, just putting it away in the hope that somehow you will feel better afterwards?

Anything and everything you can do to become more *aware* of your relationship to food and how the OEDM is using food in your day is helpful. Because I believe the basic root of overweight is *not having a proper relationship to food*.

We can believe, or people can have told us, that we are the weight we are because of genetics, because of having a slower metabolism or whatever. Although this may be somewhat true, I believe that we can all have *some sort* of influence over not only our weight but our eating and exercise patterns.

Therefore, rather than accept that the diets don't work, I hope you will feel inspired to try my method for approaching overweight. As I say elsewhere, I am only beginning to work with people in this way – but I used to be overweight myself, and my method is based on my personal experience of what it was like to live in overweight, and what helped when I started to reduce.

Because there is not the same physical shock with overweight as with underweight, people don't realise that many of the same properties are the same. Just as in underweight the EDM tells you not to eat, so in overweight it's the similar opposite.

Therefore when you hear the 'food voice' rather than think that it's you, realise it's a mechanical voice and *separate from it*. Once you become used to seeing the voice as *not the same as you*, you will have much more choice over how you approach your food.

This will start to give you a *proper relationship* to your food. Rather than acting on the OEDM's idea that the whole of your life needs to be expressed through food, you will be able to use food as it is intended – simply as fuel to enable you to get through life.

Food can still be a reward, still be fun – but it will stop being the reason why you feel the rest of your life to be disappointing, oppressive or fearful. Food is essential for life but there is more to life than food.

By understanding the concept of the OEDM, the OEDN, by separating and negotiating with the food voice, you will have a different experience of your inner self.

At the beginning this may feel fearful – but the more you begin to understand what's going on, the more the healthy side of you will become excited and hopeful about a more healthy lifestyle.

It is important not to go too far, too quickly. Sometimes losing weight can itself become a problem, as people go from one end of the line to the other end, and the EDM activates, again to try to help you, but doing it in all the wrong way – ie by anorexia or bulimia.

Instead, just as with underweight, where recovery is a gentle, fairly slow and not violent process, so with overweight losing weight involves losing weight *with the whole of your body and psyche*.

In this way, when you have achieved a weight that's better for you, there will *not* be a sense of 'cheating' or a sense that really you belong at the higher weight. So seek to *contract* your OEDN (Overweight Eating Disorder Normal) until you reach and maintain a new NN (Normal Normal).

Then with common-sense maintenance – an appropriate amount of exercise, an appropriate awareness on the food you eat – I believe you have your best chance of achieving and maintaining a healthy weight loss.

As with other aspects of therapy it's all *in the relationship*. Having been overweight – and unhappy and bullied – as a child, I never imagined I could go through life 'normally'. But discovering that there was a *relationship* between the food I was eating and my physical size meant that I could begin to influence my physical appearance and so can you.

To again restate my philosophy, this is best done gradually, and with an understanding that grows by sensible experiment and observation of what may be going on internally. Gentle exercise, increased as it feels right, and cutting out food which you know to be unhealthy is better than too rigorous a routine which can only be sustained by the action of the EDM 'waking up'. (See the early chapters on underweight to understand more about the EDM).

One of the greatest freedoms is understanding that how you have been up till now does not mean that is how you need to be from now on. Buying clothes to fit a slimmer body may help for a little while, but what will give you longer term results is under-standing that you need to *change your relationship to food*.

Finally, it's also important to recognise that, as I said at the beginning, the OEDM is a *defence mechanism* of the body. That means when you start to reduce all sorts of emotions may come to the surface. These you would do well to pay attention to, to try to smooth out what has been locked up inside the weight of your body.

This may require help from an external professional. If that's not possible, you can help yourself by talking to yourself as though you were looking at yourself objectively. We all, even if only kind-of, know what our problems are, and that is why the solutions that come from *ourselves* are the ones that will be the most meaningful.

There are always resources to help us – which can be as simple as a friend who understands and will listen to us as we sort out what our weight has meant, and how we now want to think of ourselves.

What I find as a therapist is how wonderful it is once someone starts to get interested in what's really happening inside them-selves. An elderly woman of my acquaintance used to say that when you start to discover the world inside you, what's there is *much more interesting* than the latest film, the new shoes, or reading about the lives of celebrities. Then you are no longer concerning yourself with what's out there, where you are a passive receptor of other people's lives, but you start to be excited about *what's going on inside you*. You start to have a proper relationship with your life – starting with your relationship to food.

I know this because I have been there. I have known the agony of shame, of being singled out and made fun of. Of having people call me every harsh word you could think of. The pain of not being understood, rather being ridiculed and despised.

I have known this – and I have known the dawn of joy when I started to have even the slightest hope of a proper relationship with food and with myself. And that's one thing that no one can ever deprive you of.

So why not begin? The pain of looking at yourself can be over-whelming – but at least it is pain that is trying to help you. That pain is the emotions finally hoping that they can be heard, and healed.

You will be amazed how quickly things can change – and by going at a safe pace, you will keep up with the changes.

In the next edition of this book I will have more to tell you about overweight issues. But for now, I hope I have said enough to help you begin. What happens now belongs to *you*. The end of this book can be the beginning of your new life.

CHAPTER TWELVE

Macrocosm
The Search for A
Wider Understanding

Just as not all headaches are migraines, and not every person who drinks alcohol heavily will go on to become an alcoholic, not every manifestation of eating problems is a disorder in the sense of an awakened EDM.

A concerned parent contacted me about her daughter, Rachel. Rachel had been referred to the school psychiatrist because her BMI indicated that she was in the anorexic category for her height.

It was also believed that there were some psychological issues. Questioned by the psychiatrist, Rachel admitted she had been feeling confused and isolated. Note that my use of the words 'questioned' and 'admitted' is deliberate, since although I would not couch my own work in these terms, this is how the meeting with the psychiatrist was perceived by Rachel. In other words, she was already being treated as 'a problem'.

When I spoke to Rachel she seemed more embarrassed by the fuss than embodying a life-threatening illness. Her words were 'if I thought it was going to cause all this I wouldn't have stopped eating lunch'. Once attention was focused on Rachel she found it hard to eat with her family because everyone seemed to be watching what she was eating. I suggested she be allowed to eat on her own.

Suggesting someone eats separately needs to be handled carefully. The perceived wisdom is that if the person is developing a full-blown disorder it can give them more opportunity to hide food and be harder to monitor. In Rachel's case her eating separately helped to reduce the tension she was now feeling around food. In this case it was helpful to have some flexibility in the family dynamic. She went back to eating lunch and although she said she 'missed the feeling of thinness', she remained 'herself' in that she did not begin to speak with the voice of an EDM. Within a few weeks she was back eating with the family. There were a couple of strained meals at the start but the whole family soon stopped talking about the matter, although Rachel's mother still kept a watchful, if discreet, eye on her daughter.

Pathologising a situation can be a mistake. A client of mine, Hector, reported that if his father hadn't insisted on him seeing a psychiatrist as a child he believed his childhood would have been more normal. As Hector expressed it 'when I didn't want to go to school, rather than being sent for a psychiatric evaluation, my father should have just insisted I behave'. By trying to bring in the experts to help Hector, his father made him overly self-conscious. An eating disorder developed in late adolescence. Hector still wonders if it could have been prevented by a more natural response to what was no more than unusual but not impossible childhood behaviour?

For a while it has been believed that an eating disorder is 'a family problem' and some analysts prefer to work with the whole family to bring about a recovery in one of the members (Selvini-Palazzoli, 1974; Minuchin,1978). As always, if we are considering The Matthew Method, what needs to be added to whatever approach being used is the understanding that the EDM and OEDM are a specific, mechanical function. Otherwise the success/failure of the family therapy will be being judged by an incomplete understanding, and family members may finish up shouldering the blame for something that in reality centres around a dysfunctioning body defence mechanism.

A while ago, responding to my website, a woman contacted me concerning her daughter. The family lives on the Isle of Wight and there was no way they could visit me in person. Talking on the phone to Wendy, the mother, I was immediately struck by her sense of guilt. She came across as a warm, particularly dynamic individual who clearly felt devastated that she had somehow got it wrong.

The first thing I noticed was how she talked. 'We are going to beat this thing!' she said. Beginning my response there, I highlighted her use of the term 'we' in order to make her aware of how she had automatically taken on an inappropriate responsibility. '*You* can't, Wendy, because *you* don't have the disorder – Liz does'.

There was a shocked silence from the other side. It turned out that Wendy and Liz had been in contact with their local hospital for over a month and this was the first time anyone had contradicted the way she was speaking about Liz's situation. Wendy said that she could see that her approach may have needlessly confused the central issue, since it had led to Liz having to take on the extra burden of Wendy's over-involvement.

There is also the example of my bulimic client who was quite able to put on a half-stone 'by eating crap' – junk / snack food. The fact that he was able to put on a half-stone did not indicate that anything specific had happened to alleviate the nature of his disorder. It merely meant that the disorder better tolerated that sort of non-nurturing food. If weight is going to be the sole or predominant factor guiding 'recovery', then it may be that traditional methods of recovery are leaving themselves wide open to the sort of cunning the EDM practices in appearing to be 'defeated'.

The whole emphasis I place with my clients is on careful, gentle, recovery over a period of time. And remember that rather than expensive institutionalised treatment, my clients come to me for at the most two sessions a week. With the current NHS demands for 'quick treatment' it's important to remember that the disorder has taken time to evolve and will need time to disentangle. But with my approach, time needn't be expensive because it can be fitted round the rest of the working or school week.

Most people I encounter who have had some experience within the more general world of disorder recovery have reported feeling beaten into submission and made to feel guilty or shamed for their disorder. Clearly this book has been written to provide new information, and the hope is that concerned experts in all fields will find cause to integrate their current practice with the different angle in this book to working with people with disorders – one that understands the *difference* between the person and their disorder, and concentrates on supporting the patient while they detach from their own EDM.

The treatment of eating disorders, as my correspondent notes in Chapter 1, can sometimes seem to be rooted in a lack of perception. Not only is the true nature of the EDM not understood, but the person is seen as being deliberately wilful, and the treatment that follows can be 'tit for tat'. To witness or to hear about the experience of a child or adolescent, brought before a panel of 'experts' and made to feel humiliated for having 'failed' (ie they vomited or did not eat their food) is a sad and disheartening experience for anyone concerned with healing and support.

In her section on Supervision, Shipton addresses this issue. 'Psychotherapists and counsellors are used to having regular consultative meetings with senior colleagues where they discuss their clinical work. This kind of supervision is essential, especially as the counter-transference impact of people with eating disorders is considerable. Other professions do not necessarily regularly have such support, but may benefit enormously from the opportunity to discuss their work with someone who can understand the stresses and strains of multi-disciplinary working with people with eating disorders...

'As mentioned earlier the unconscious splitting and divisive processes that can be mobilised by patients are formidable. Furthermore, there will always be some members of staff who are uncomfortable with their own relationship with food and to their body and their anxieties can also easily be mobilised.

'In specialist agencies there may well be a number of very difficult patients, some with borderline personality disorder, and the emotional turbulence that they create can be overwhelming. The fear of losing patients who are starving to death or acting out in dangerous ways can create burnout in dedicated professionals' (Shipton, ibid, 109-110).

Rightly, Shipton is highlighting the confrontative aspect of particularly anorexic patients, and to this can be added the effect of witnessing a bulimic patient's purging.

As I have already stated, one aspect of my writing this book is to offer something different and new to professionals in the field of eating disorders. I hope passionately that it will not be enough to read this book and think: 'Yes that's an interesting idea – but we'll keep doing things the way we always have'. I am not saying that nobody has ever made a complete recovery and that only my approach is at all viable, but there is a fundamental difference in my approach which I do believe needs to be considered and hopefully *integrated* into current medical and psychological practice.

I am certain, from what I have read in their own books, that many people are genuinely and wholeheartedly struggling to come to terms with understanding the devastating nature of what we term an 'eating disorder'. There is great good in their intentions although sometimes they must feel disheartened by the failures. I would hope these good people may read what is written in this book and incorporate it into their own work.

As I was finishing this text, I was contacted by two women, just finishing degrees in counselling. They had read about my work on my website and we met for a couple of hours. Afterwards one of them wrote to me:

'Matthew,

I got so much out of our meeting. It was so significant that the three of us had shared the experience of having had an eating disorder and survived .... Knowing this gave me a deeper connection with you, Matthew. I remember saying how stimulated I had felt to listen to your thinking with respect to eating disorders.

This contrasted with the other two interviews I had had. In one I had felt 'full up' when the nurse had shared their eating plan with me. I was sickened at the thought of all the calories they wanted to pump into their patients when their body weight was so frail and their minds so petrified. There was a sense for me that they were being punished for not eating.

This felt like there was too much emphasis on the food, It felt barbaric.... At last here was someone who felt and thought the same as I did, based on my own experience. Someone who preferred another way to the terrifying method of force feeding. Someone who so respected the client that instead of the dreaded food, he offered little bits of information, something that is easy to digest'. (Personal communication, 2007)

When someone is faced with a child or adolescent who is starving the urge to force re-feed may be great. I would hope that what has been set out in this book will provide the answer to what should then happen. What is important is understanding, both from the expert and the person with the illness. It is agonising to hear of children having to hide their vomit in socks so as not to be exposed by members of staff. Or weeping alone in the night, terrified not only of what is inside them, but of the anger it brings out in those empowered with treating them. Surely there has to be the recognition that it's 'not normal' behaviour – so the idea of *something else* driving the behaviour surely makes better sense?

Particularly with a child since they are thought of as not being able to control themselves, so naturally what little self-reliance they have is taken away from them. It may be thought that a disadvantage of my approach is it relies on the person being able to *understand* what is going on. That children under a certain age would not be capable of processing the information concerning the EDM.

Yet Melanie Klein used to psychoanalyse children as little as three. A child of seven, the age at which hospitals are now seeing children with anorexia, is perfectly capable of understanding, for example, the Sorcerer's Apprentice story. By introducing this story to the child and explaining that *this* is what is going on inside, the child will get a simple understanding of what they can do to bring about their own recovery.

I remember in my own recovery understanding that being at peace with my EDM was a better way to achieve recovery than hating it. Accepting that it is there, like acceptance generally, removes the *conflict* that makes things harder. Of course, 'being at peace' is very different from 'pro' anorexia and bulimia sites where usually adolescent girls and some boys encourage each other to 'worship the goddess of anorexia'. They are engaged in their own struggle – and perhaps this book will find a way to reach them as well.

Whether or not, as is being argued in the press, we are seeing a growth in the number of cases of eating disorders, or whether the statement makes perfect sense since there is more and more alienation in childhood, eating disorders have become as much of our day by day experience as Aids was in the 1980s. Perhaps with the right method, as occurred with Aids, the illness can be contained although not eradicated. Just as Aids is an auto-immune deficiency, so eating disorders come from within – perhaps they are a new 'cancer' – one that can be cured with understanding.

And just as it took time to come to the right approach to combat Aids, so I write this book to add new information to the understanding of the nature of and recovery from an eating disorder.

The percentage of people with eating disorders who never recover, who either live uncomfortably with the illness, or who die, is far too high. Of course, even a single person lost to the illness is one too many. However I have heard evidence of a sense of acceptance of the losses, a feeling that nothing can be done and that's all there is to say.

I cannot be so sanguine. The words of John Donne, writing in the 17th century, came with force into my mind and have lodged there as a wake-up call and a vision for a world in which people are not lost to eating disorders:

'Each man's death diminishes me, for I am intimately connected with mankind. Therefore do not send to know for whom the bell tolls, it tolls for thee'.

Just as the illness, like rust, never sleeps, so surely our response to the illness can never sleep, never be complacent. Human beings, as a race, as a whole, have been given a new challenge. With humility, courage and determination we must put aside ego, let go of what does not help all who are affected, and find a way through. It is not only for those who are suffering, it is for the rest of us. We are being asked to look at something in a new way. I hope that we can.

REFERENCES

Athanassiou, C Journal of Child Psychotherapy, 11 (2), pp 5-19, 1985

Austin, S B. Fat, loathing and public health. Culture, Medicine and Psychiatry, 23, pp 245 – 268 1999

Barnett, L. Journal of Child Psychotherapy 5, pp 47-55, 1979

Bentovim, M. Anorexia nervosa and relating eating disorders in childhood and adolescence. Hove, Psychology press, 2000

Bidgood, Jacqueline & Buckroyd, Julia. An exploration of obese adults' experience of attempting to lose weight and to maintain a reduced weight. Counselling & Psychotherapy Research. BACP Publications 2005

Bion, WR. Learning from Experience. Karnac Books 1962

Birksted-Breen, D. International Journal of Psycho-Analysis, 70, pp 29-40 1989

Britton, R S. The Oedipus Complex Today. Pp 83-101. Karnac Books 1989

Britton, R S. Belief and Imagination. Pp 41-58. London, Routledge 1998

Bruch, H. Eating Disorders. London, Routledge and Kegan Paul, 1974

Bruch, H. The Golden Cage. London, Open Books 1978

Bruch, H. Psychotherapy in Eating Disorders. Canadian Psychiatric Association Journal. 22 (3) pp 102-108 1977

Burgner, M. Female experience. Pp 93-103. Rutledge 1997

Campling, M. A DIY Cure for Anorexia. Therapy Today magazine. BACP Publications 2006

Campling, M. Chapter on Eating Disorders in Client Centred Practice. PCCS Books 2007

Dare, C. The Starving and the Greedy. Journal of Child Psychotherapy 19(2) pp3-22. 1993

De Mille, A. Martha, the life and work of Martha Graham. Hutchinson 1991

Dolan, B & Gitzinger, I (editors) Why Women? Athlone Press 1994

Farrell, E. Lost for Words. Process Press 1995

Fraiberg, S H. Ghosts in the nursery. Journal of Child Psychiatry 14, pp 387-421 1975

Hart, M. Act One. Secker & Warburg 1961

Holford, Patrick. The New Optimum Nutrition Bible. Piatkus Books 2004

Klein, M. Envy and Gratitude. Vintage 1997

Klein, M. The Development of a Child. Love Guilt and Reparation. Vintage 1975

Lawrence, M. The Anorexic Experience. Women's Press 1984

Lawrence, M & Dana, M. Understanding bulimia. Social Work and the legacy of Freud. Basingstoke, MacMillan 1988

Lawrence, M. Fed up and Hungry. London, The Women's Press 1987

Likierman, M Journal of Child Psychotherapy 23 pp 61-80 1997

McDougall, J. Theatres of the Body. London, Free Association Books 1989

Magagna, J. Anorexia nervosa and related eating disorders in childhood and adolescence. Pp 227-263 Hove, Psychology Press 2000

Meltzer, D. Explorations in Autism. Pp 223-238, Strath, Tay, Clunie Press 1975

Milner, M The suppressed madness of sane men. Pp 21-38 London, Tavistock Publications 1987

Minuchin, S, Roseman BL and Baker L. Psychosomatic Families: Anorexia Nervosa in Context. Harvard University Press 1978

Orbach, S. Fat is a Feminist Issue. Arrow 1987

Ouspensky, P. In Search of the Miraculous. Routledge Kegan Paul, 1950

Pagels, Elaine. The Gnostic Gospels. Vintage Books 1979

Selvini-Palazzoli, M, 1974. Self-Starvation: from the Individual to Family Therapy in the Treatment of Anorexia Nervosa. Reprinted, 1978 New York Jason Aronson

Rey, H. Universals in psychoanalysis in the treatment of psychotic and borderline states. London, Free Association books 1994

Rhode, M. Going to Pieces. Psychotic states in children pp 231-244. London, Duckworth 1997

Richards et al. Adventure Therapy and Eating Disorders, A Feminist Approach to Research and Practice. Brathay 2001

Rogers, Carl. Client-Centered Therapy. Constable 1951

Shipton, Geraldine. Working with Eating Disorders. Palgrave (MacMillan) 2004

Sylvester, E. Psychoanalytic Study of the child 1, pp 167-187 1970

Williams, Gianna. Internal Landscapes and Foreign Bodies. London, Duckworth 1997

Williams, G, Williams, P, Desmarais, J, Ravenscroft, K. The Generosity of Acceptance. Vol 1 & Vol 2. London Karnac 2004

Winnicott, Donald. Playing and Reality. Tavistock Publications 1971

6 Malvern Terrace

Islington

London N1 1HR

Printed in the United Kingdom
by Lightning Source UK Ltd.
125252UK00001B/418-618/A